AIR WAR
AT NIGHT

AIR WAR AT NIGHT

The
battle for
the night
sky since
1915

ROBERT JACKSON

Airlife

England

Copyright © 2000 Robert Jackson

First published in the UK in 2000
by Airlife Publishing Ltd

British Library Cataloguing-in-Publication Data
A catalogue reord for this book
is available from the British Library

ISBN 1 84037 100 5

Typeset by Servis Filmsetting Ltd, Manchester
Printed in China

Airlife Publishing Ltd
101 Longden Road, Shrewsbury, SY3 9EB, England
E-mail: airlife@airlifebooks.com
Website: www.airlifebooks.com

CONTENTS

CHAPTER ONE

THE FIRST BLITZ ON BRITAIN, 1915–18

A Maurice Farman of No 3 Squadron RFC made the first night flight by a military aircraft in Britain on 16 April 1913. (Philip Jarrett)

By the outbreak of World War I in August 1914, the threat of air attack on the British Isles was being taken very seriously by both the War Office and the Admiralty – especially the latter, which viewed Germany's Zeppelin airships as a considerable menace to the Royal Navy's vital dockyards. In theory it was the Royal Flying Corps, under the direction of the War Office, that bore the responsibility for the air defence of Great Britain, but the RFC had no aircraft or funds available for home defence.

The problem had not escaped the attention of the First Sea Lord, Winston Churchill, who in 1912 initiated the establishment of a chain of coastal aerodromes for use by aircraft working with ships at sea, or for air defence. In November 1913, after a great deal of wrangling, it was agreed that while the War Office retained overall responsibility for the air defence of Britain, the Admiralty, through the Naval Wing of the RFC (which was to reform as the Royal Naval Air Service on 1 July 1914) was to be responsible for the protection of naval bases.

It must be said that the Military Wing of the RFC, right up to the outbreak of war, had given little thought to the development of aircraft as an armed weapon of war, regarding it primarily as a reconnaissance tool. At the end of 1913, on the other hand, the Admiralty had issued a requirement for a 'home service fighting machine to repel enemy aircraft'. But it was the Military Wing that first demonstrated the feasibility of operating aircraft at night; on 16 April 1913 Lieutenant R. Cholmondeley of No 3 Squadron flew a Maurice Farman from Larkhill to Upavon and back by moonlight, and in June Lieutenant G.I. Carmichael took off and landed with the aid of petrol flares on the ground.

Experimental in nature though they still were, the German Navy's Zeppelins were beginning to prove their worth in North Sea reconnaissance operations by the end of 1914, and a plan now formed to extend their role to offensive operations over the British Isles. The plan had actually originated some three weeks after the war began, but it had been shelved because the handful of Navy airships available during the last months of 1914 were fully committed to patrol and reconnaissance duties.

On 25 December 1914 the German Army used its small fleet of airships to raid the French towns of Nancy, Dunkirk and Verdun. The Navy immediately requested the release of its own airships to attack selected targets on the east coast of England, but the request was turned down by the Navy Minister, *Grossadmiral* von Tirpitz, who believed that the bombing of these targets by single airships would have little or no material effect. He advised *Admiral* Hugo von Pohl, the Chief of Naval Staff, to defer such a move until both Army and Navy were in a position to mount a maximum-effort raid on London with all available airships.

Another serious obstacle to the Navy's plans at this time was the *Kaiser* himself, who was unwilling to authorise the bombing of targets in Britain, and particularly in London. It all added up to frustration for the planning staff of the Naval Airship Division. By the middle of December the division had enough airships to carry out both the primary task of reconnaissance in co-operation with the High Seas Fleet and long-range special missions over England, and every delay in obtaining authority to undertake the latter type of operation meant that favourable weather conditions were being allowed to slip by. There was also the danger that the Navy's new airships might be destroyed in enemy air attacks before they could be used to good effect, and this fear was expressed in a letter to von Pohl from *Konteradmiral* Philipp, the Chief of German Naval Aviation. There had already been a British air attack on the German Navy's airship facilities. On 21 November, three Avro 504s of the RNAS, flying from Belfort and piloted by Squadron Commander E.F. Briggs, Flight Lieutenant J.T. Babington and Lieutenant S.V. Sippe, had bombed the Zeppelin sheds at Friedrichshafen, where the airships were manufactured. A gas tank was set on fire and Zeppelin L7 (LZ32) slightly damaged. This was followed by a second raid on 24 December, when aircraft of the RNAS were launched by seaplane carriers in the German Bight to attack Zeppelin sheds at Nordholz, in northern Germany. On this occasion, no damage was caused.

More importantly, on this same day a Friedrichshafen FF29 seaplane of the Imperial German Navy's *Seeflieger Abteilung* 1 (Seaplane Detachment 1) dropped the first bomb on British soil, in the garden of an auctioneer living near Dover Castle. There were no casualties and little damage. On Christmas Day the same aircraft and crew dropped two bombs near Cliffe railway station, Kent. The FF29 was intercepted by a Vickers Gunbus of No 7 Squadron RFC and several bursts were fired at it, but it got away.

Pressure from Philipp and other senior naval commanders eventually resulted in von Pohl seeking an audience with the *Kaiser* on 7 January 1915, in which the *admiral* stressed the importance of attacking military objectives in England during the months of January and February, when weather conditions for long-range airship operations would be at their best.

Reluctantly, the *Kaiser* gave his consent to air attacks on the docks and military installations on the lower Thames and the east coast of England –

but not on London. After months of waiting, the Airship Division could at last go ahead with its plan, already worked out in minute detail by *Korvettenkapitän* Peter Strasser, commanding the Naval Airship Division. The plan, submitted to von Pohl on 10 January 1915 for his final approval, envisaged attacks on Tynemouth, the Humber, Great Yarmouth, Lowestoft, Harwich and the Thames Estuary by three airships, which would bomb their targets at dusk after a daylight flight over the North Sea and return to their bases under cover of darkness.

The first attack, made on the night of 19/20 January 1915, was abortive in that no military targets were hit, although two airships penetrated into Norfolk and dropped their bombs in the vicinity of Great Yarmouth and King's Lynn, causing some £8,000-worth of damage and killing four people, one a small boy. Further attempts, made by Army airships during the next two months, were also abortive.

The north experienced its first Zeppelin attack on the night of 14/15 April 1915. Earlier, the naval airship L9, commanded by *Kapitänleutnant* Heinrich Mathy, had set out on a reconnaissance flight to the west of Terschelling. She carried ten 110 lb high explosive (HE) and 40 incendiary bombs, and after flying all day without sighting any British ships Mathy obtained permission to carry out a raid on a British coastal target before returning to base. The objective selected by Mathy was Tynemouth, with its complex of shipyards, but landfall was made at Blyth, some miles to the north, and the L9's commander mistook the Wansbeck for the Tyne. Most of his bombs fell harmlessly in open country around the area's mining villages, although two people were injured at Wallsend when a near miss damaged their house. Convinced that he had inflicted considerable damage on the Tyne's shipyards, Mathy set course for home. A solitary Bristol TB8 took off from the Royal Naval Air Station at Whitley Bay, established six weeks earlier to counter Zeppelin attacks on the Tynemouth area, and patrolled at 5,000 feet over Newcastle for an hour, unassisted by any searchlights and without sighting the enemy. Its pilot, Sub-Lieutenant P. Legh, had never before flown at night. The TB8's gunner was a young Australian named Bert Hinkler, who later trained as a pilot and became famous for making the first solo flight from England to Australia in 1928.

At this time the air defence of Great Britain was the sole responsibility of the RNAS, mainly because the RNAS had more aircraft available than the RFC. Most of the naval aircraft assigned to air defence, however, were concentrated in the home counties and East Anglia, as were the relatively few anti-aircraft guns and searchlights, so that the

North's defences were minimal. The Whitley Bay station, for example, had three aircraft (two of which were unserviceable) at the time of the L9's incursion, and its weaponry comprised a few carbines with 209 incendiary rounds between them, twenty-four Hale rifle grenades without the rifles to fire them, and twenty Hale incendiary bombs with only one set of dropping gear.

On 16/17 May, for the first time, an airship was illuminated by a defending searchlight. She was *Hauptmann* Linnarz's LZ38, which dropped thirty-three bombs in the Dover area before making off. It was also the first time, thanks to the searchlights, that a Zeppelin was seen by defending pilots, but the three defence sorties by RNAS pilots from Dover and Westgate failed to come anywhere near her.

On the night of 31 May/1 June 1915 Linnarz led

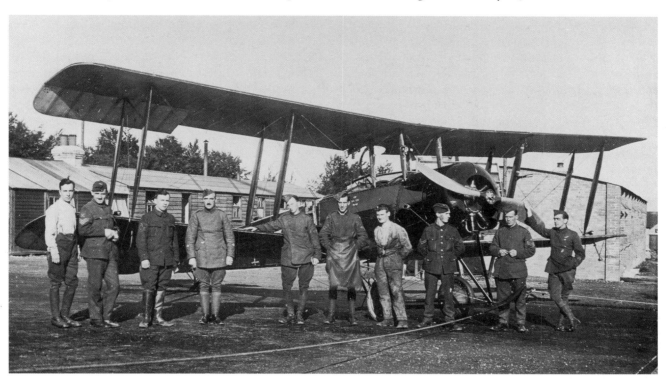

Top and above: *The Avro 504 was one of the types used in attempts to intercept the early Zeppelin raids. It was also used by the RNAS to attack Zeppelin sheds.* (Philip Jarrett)

11

the first attack on London, LZ38 being joined by LZ39. Fifteen defence sorties were flown from Chingford, Eastchurch, Hendon, Rochford and Westgate, all by RNAS aircraft. Seven different aircraft types were involved; there was no co-ordination, and there were several landing accidents, one of them fatal.

On the night of 6 June Heinrich Mathy's L9 was once again active over the north, and this time the target was Hull. The Zeppelin dropped ten HE and fifty incendiary bombs, killing twenty-four people, injuring forty, and causing nearly £45,000-worth of damage. Naval aircraft took off from Killingholme and Yarmouth, but failed to make contact. Three Army Zeppelins which set out to raid London on this night failed to reach the English coast for various reasons, and one of them, LZ37, was destroyed over Belgium by Flight Sub-Lieutenant Reginald Warneford, flying a Morane Parasol, who dropped six 20 lb bombs on it after a chase lasting an hour. The encounter was accidental, as Warneford had been *en route* to attack the airship shed at Berchem Ste Agathe, but it proved that the Zeppelin was vulnerable to air attack provided the attacking aircraft had the advantage of height. In this case Warneford, who coaxed his Morane up to 11,000 feet, sighted the airship as it was passing through 7,000 feet, descending towards its base at Evère. A second airship, LZ38, was destroyed soon after docking at Evère when its shed was bombed by pilots of No 1 RNAS Squadron, based in France.

Following the loss of the two Army ships a tentative plan by the Navy to position its own airships at forward bases in Belgium was abandoned, and the next raid on Britain was made from Nordholz on the night of 15 June by the L10 commanded by *Kapitänleutnant* Hirsch. The L10 was an improved type of Zeppelin and was the forerunner of nine more airships of a similar class, all with a capacity of 1,126,000 cubic feet, which would be bought by the Navy before the end of 1915. The ships were 536 feet long and were powered by four 210 hp Maybach engines. They could cruise at 11,000 feet and fly as far as the west coast of England with a two-ton bomb load.

The L10's target on this June night was Tyneside. Hirsch crossed the coast near Blyth at a quarter to midnight, turned south, and for half an hour dropped 3,500 lb of bombs on Wallsend, Jarrow and South Shields, killing eighteen people, injuring seventy-two and causing damage amounting to nearly £42,000. No warning of the raid had been received, and much of the target area was brightly lit. Two sorties by BE2 aircraft were flown from Whitley Bay, but no contact was made. As a result of this raid, the Tyneside garrison commander advised Major-General H.M. Lawson, the GOC-in-C Northern Command, that the naval aircraft at Whitley Bay were inadequate for the defence task, and that an additional air station at Gosforth would be an advantage. The recommendation was approved, and a small RNAS detachment under Lieutenant Christopher Draper was operational there in July.

The next attack on the north, on the night of 9/10 August, was intended as a diversion for a major raid on London, which in the event was a dismal failure. The northern raider was once again the old L9, commanded this time by *Kapitänleutnant* Odo Loewe, who crossed the coast near Hornsea and bombed Goole in the belief that it was Hull. Air defence sorties were flown from Hornsea racecourse, Redcar – where there was a naval flying training establishment – and Whitley Bay, but although the L9 was sighted by pilots from Hornsea she was not engaged and escaped in thick mist.

On 7/8 September 1915 it was once again the Army's turn to raid London. The ships involved were the LZ74, LZ77 and the Schutte-Lanz SL2. The latter bombed Millwall, Deptford, Greenwich and Woolwich docks, causing a great deal of damage. Targets in England were attacked again on the following night, but only one ship managed to reach London; she was the L13, with Mathy in command, and her bombs started a huge fire among the textile warehouses to the north of St Paul's. In this one raid, Mathy caused one-sixth of the total damage inflicted on Britain during all the air raids of World War I; the total loss amounted to over half a million pounds.

Odo Loewe and the L9 returned to the north on the night of 8 September, crossing the coast near Whitby at 21.15 to raid the ironworks at Skinningrove. The attack was made with great accuracy but little damage was done, and the Zeppelin was well clear of the area before the first aircraft – a BE2 from Redcar – arrived on the scene. This was the last attack made on the north in 1915, and raids on southern England petered out a month later. For the remaining weeks of the year, the Navy's Zeppelins were either employed on co-operation work with the Fleet or were grounded by bad weather. When operations began again in January 1916, they were directed against targets spread along the whole length of England. The first raid of the year, on the last night of January, was a deep-penetration mission against Liverpool by nine Zeppelins. Twenty-two air defence sorties were flown without result, but one airship, the L19, came down in the North Sea through a combination of engine trouble and rifle fire from the Dutch Friesian Islands and was lost with all her crew, including her commander, Odo Loewe.

During 1915, it had become increasingly apparent that the RNAS was ill-equipped to deal with the Zeppelin threat, and it was clear that if matters were

Insert and above: *The BE2e/d variants proved quite successful in the anti-Zeppelin campaign if pilots had sufficient time to gain height and get above the airship to make their attack. Otherwise, they could be easily outclimbed.* (Philip Jarrett)

to improve the Royal Flying Corps, which had assisted the RNAS to a limited extent in the course of the year, would have to become much more involved, even to the extent of assuming the air defence commitment in full. The Admiralty and the War Office, however, found it hard to agree on anything, beyond the fundamental facts that Zeppelins were difficult to find in the dark and that night flying was fraught with peril, so while very brave young men in wholly inadequate aircraft were striving to confront the enemy, another war was being waged in Whitehall – a prolonged and unseemly wrangle over the responsibility for Britain's air defence.

In June 1915, the Director of Home Defence, General Launcelot Kiggell, had proposed that the Navy deal with enemy aircraft approaching the coast and that the Army take over once the enemy had come inland; this was firmed up by the Army Council in November, but it was not until 10 February 1916 that a formal agreement to this effect was endorsed by the War Committee. With effect from 12 noon on 16 February, 1916, the Commander-in-Chief Home Forces was to assume responsibility for the defence of London, and for the rest of the country on the 22nd.

Meanwhile, by prior agreement with the RNAS, the RFC had positioned three BE2cs at Cramlington on 1 December 1915 for the defence of Tyneside, and on 18 March 1916 these formed the nucleus of the newly-formed No 36 Squadron, the first RFC squadron formed for the specific task of home defence. Flights were quickly established at Ashington, Hylton and Seaton Carew. Later in March, for the air defence of the southern part of the region, No 33 Squadron was transferred from Filton to Beverley in Yorkshire, with a detached flight at Bramham Moor, Tadcaster. In September 1916 No 76 Squadron formed at Ripon, with detached flights at Copmanthorpe, Helperby and Catterick, and in the following month No 77 Squadron was established at Edinburgh, with flights at Whiteburn, New Hagerston and Penston. By the end of the year, therefore, the north was defended by four front-line squadrons, all equipped with BE2 and, later, BE12 aircraft. Between them they had at their disposal no less than thirty-four landing grounds between Humber and Tyne and thirty-five between Tyne and Forth.

Despite these deployments, no raider was

13

BE2c 2473 Nightdress *of No 51 Squadron RFC, a Home Defence unit based at Thetford in Norfolk. The aircraft was written off on 29 July 1916. The squadron apparently had four named aircraft, the others being* Nighthawk, Nightclub *and* Nightmare. (Philip Jarrett)

The BE12 was widely used as a night fighter in WWI. This aircraft (6510), piloted by 2nd Lt (later AVM) W.A. McLaughry, was one of two flown from Dover on 12 August 1916. This later photograph shows the aircraft after a landing accident. Note the Le Prieur rocket rails. (Philip Jarrett)

destroyed by the northern air defences in the course of seven attacks that were made on targets from the Forth to the Humber between the beginning of March and the end of September 1916. Deployment of anti-aircraft weaponry to the north was still painfully slow, and it took a particularly costly raid on Hull on the night of 5 March 1916, after which a mob smashed up a vehicle belonging to the RFC, to bring about the hasty installation of two thirteen-pounder, two three-inch, one twelve-pounder and one six-pounder guns, while at the same time the defences around the Humber and along the east coast were generally strengthened.

Meanwhile, on 1 February 1916, the various air defence detachments in the London area had been brought together under No 19 Reserve Aeroplane Squadron, a newly-formed unit with its HQ at Hounslow. On 25 March the London defences were again reorganised and placed under the new No 18 Wing, and on 15 April No 19 RAS became No 39 (Home Defence) Squadron.

At the beginning of June 1916 eight RFC squadrons were dedicated to home defence. These were No 28 at Gosport and Newhaven; No 33 at Bramham Moor, Coal Aston, Beverley and Doncaster; No 36 at Cramlington, Turnhouse and Seaton Carew; No 39 at Hounslow, Hainault Farm, Sutton's Farm and North Weald; No 50 at Dover and Wye; No 51 at Thetford, Norwich and Narborough; No 52 at Hounslow, Goldhanger and Rochford; and No 54 at Castle Bromwich, Lilbourne, Papplewick and Waddington. Between them, they had an established aircraft strength of 134; their actual strength was sixty. At the same time, 271 anti-aircraft guns and 258 searchlights were available for the defence of key points, against a requirement of 487 and 490 respectively.

While the RFC strove to achieve some form of effective night defence organisation, a warning system was established and observer posts set up all over the country. These were connected with warning control centres and gradually began to prove their worth. Girls' names were used to identify individual Zeppelins, which were listed in alphabetical order as they crossed the coast. One of the first lines of defence against the incoming Zeppelins was the interception of their wireless traffic by direction-finding stations, and by the end of 1916 a network of huge sound locator mirrors, some built into cliffs, had also been set up.

By August 1916 the squadrons of the Home Defence Wing had adopted a system whereby aircraft operating from the landing grounds around the country were assigned individual patrol areas which overlapped, so that if a Zeppelin was sighted mutual support was readily available – at least in theory. Although aircrews had now amassed a considerable amount of experience in night operations, and were aware that night flying held no special complications, the Zeppelins remained notoriously hard to locate without searchlight assistance, anti-aircraft shellbursts or marker rockets, the latter fired by the coastal observers.

Then there were the allied problems of armament and interception techniques. Because the Zeppelin presented so vast a target, the favoured method of attack was from above, using small bombs, either the 20 lb Hale or the 60 lb incendiary designed at the Royal Laboratory, Woolwich, but there were alternative weapons. One was the Ranken Dart, devised by Engineer Lieutenant Francis Ranken, RN. Originally used by the RNAS, and also adopted by the RFC, the dart weighed about one pound and consisted of an iron-pointed metal tube containing high explosive and black powder. The tail unit embodied spring-loaded vanes which opened and locked into position to engage the Zeppelin's envelope after the head had penetrated inside, and at the same time activated a detonator rod. The dart, held fast to the envelope, would then burst into flames, igniting the gas from the airship's ruptured cells. The darts were carried in batches of twenty-four, which could be released all at once or in small groups.

Another anti-Zeppelin weapon was the Fiery Grapnel, which was carried in pairs attached to a BE2c. The idea was to approach the Zeppelin from right angles with the grapnel trailing behind, then to leap over the intended victim and allow the weapon to engage its envelope, whereupon an explosive charge would ignite leaking hydrogen.

The problem with these devices was that, because of the Zeppelin's superior rate of climb, it was usually difficult, if not impossible, for an attacking aircraft to get above it. The answer, clearly, was to be able to attack from any position, including below, using incendiary bullets.

Such bullets had existed for some years. One had been invented by a New Zealander, John Pomeroy, in 1908 and had been offered without success to the British government in 1914; it was only in 1916, after Pomeroy had written to David Lloyd George, that the Munitions Inventions Department agreed to sponsor development. In August that year, an order for half a million rounds was placed on behalf of the RFC.

The Admiralty had shown more interest in an explosive bullet designed by Flight Lieutenant F.A. Brock, and this was also ordered for both the RNAS and RFC, as was a phosphorus incendiary bullet designed by a Coventry engineer, J.F. Buckingham. This mixture of bullets was on issue to the home defence squadrons by the end of August 1916.

The result was immediate, and dramatic. On the night of 2 September, the Army's Schutte-Lanz airship SL11 (*Hauptmann* Wilhelm Schramm) was

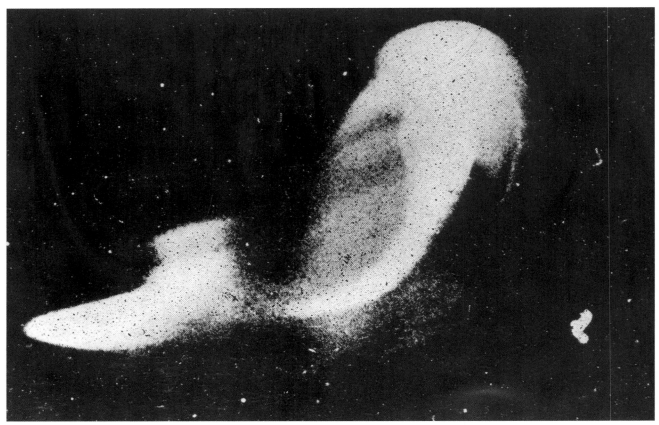

The fiery end of Heinrich Mathy's L31, shot down in flames at Potter's Bar by Lt W.J. Tempest, RFC. The blazing mass has already broken in two. (Author)

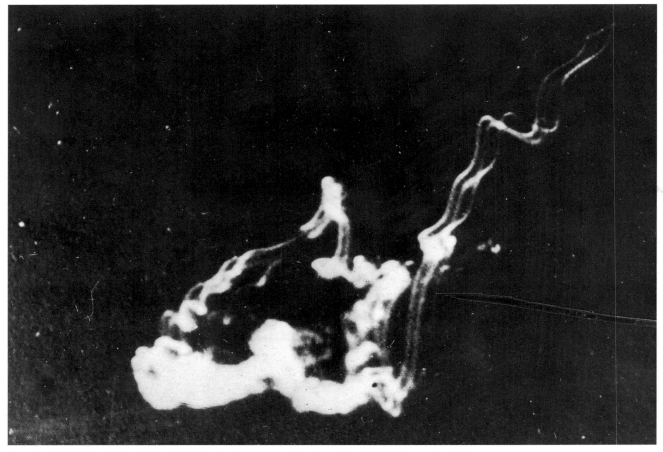

16 | *Zeppelin L34 (Kaptlt Max Dietrich) falling in flames over Hartlepool Bay, 28/29 November 1916.* (Author)

shot down in flames at Cuffley by Lieutenant William Leefe Robinson of No 39 Squadron. On 22 September L32 (*Oberleutnant-zur-See* Werner Peterson) fell in flames over Essex after being attacked by 2nd Lieutenant Frederick Sowrey, while Alois Bocker's L33 crash-landed near Little Wigborough, having suffered severe damage from anti-aircraft fire and the efforts of Lieutenant Alfred Brandon of 39 Squadron. Finally, on 1 October, one of a force of eleven Zeppelins that set out to raid England was shot down over Potter's Bar by 2nd Lieutenant W.J. Tempest. She was the L31, commanded by Heinrich Mathy.

All these successes had been in the south. But on the night of 28/29 November the northern air defences at last had their chance. Zeppelin L34, *Kapitänleutnant* Max Dietrich, was shot down off the coast by 2nd Lieutenant Ian Pyott of No 36 Squadron, flying a BE2c from Seaton Carew, soon after bombing targets in south-east Durham. All twenty crew perished. Another airship, the L21, was also destroyed that night by naval pilots from Great Yarmouth.

Although there were to be further Zeppelin attacks on the United Kingdom before the war's end, from May 1917 the emphasis switched to attacks on London and the south-east by heavier-than-air bombers, first by day and later by night. The principal bomber involved was the Gotha GIV,

which could carry a typical war load of six 110 lb bombs. Its maximum speed was about 85 mph, which even so was faster than some of the fighter aircraft sent up to intercept it, and its attack altitude of 16,000 feet made it a difficult target, unless defensive fighters had ample warning of its approach. The first attack on the British mainland, mounted by twenty-three Gothas in daylight on 25 May 1917, killed ninety-five civilians and injured 195 in Folkestone. More than seventy home defence aircraft were sent up to intercept, but the only ones to make contact were flown by two ferry pilots. Several Gothas were destroyed in subsequent raids, but these mostly fell to anti-aircraft fire or failed to regain their base because of adverse weather. The few home defence aircraft that did get close enough to intercept were usually beaten off by the Gotha's substantial defensive armament of three Spandau machine-guns.

In September 1917 the Gothas switched to night attacks, and they were now joined by an even more formidable bomber: the Zeppelin (*Staaken*) R Type, known as the *Riesenflugzeug* (giant aircraft). This monster was capable of carrying a 2,200 lb bomb at 14,000 feet at 80 mph under the power of its four 260 hp Mercedes engines; moreover, it was defended by five machine-guns, which made it a much tougher target than the Gotha. Only a small number of R Types were built, but they presented

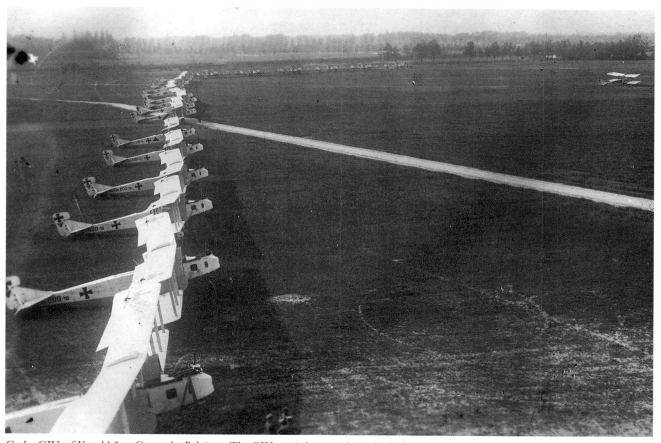

Gotha GIVs of Kagohl 3 at Gontrode, Belgium. The GIV carried a typical war load of six 110 lb bombs. (Philip Jarrett)

17

The Zeppelin (Staaken) *R Type posed problems for the air defences. It was heavily armed and presented a difficult target for attacking fighters.* (Philip Jarrett)

an immense threat to British targets.

To meet this threat, the War Office implemented a new defence scheme whereby anti-aircraft guns and patrolling aircraft were allocated separate operating zones. In addition, balloons trailing steel cable 'curtains' floated in barriers up to 8,000 feet, theoretically forcing any attacking aircraft to fly above that height to a level where fighters would be patrolling. Sound locators – simple trumpet devices at first, followed by more sophisticated fixed sound mirrors – were also playing their part by the end of 1917. The first sound mirror, a fifteen-foot reflector cut into the chalk cliff at Fan Bay, east of Dover, and focused on a point midway between Dunkirk and Calais, was operational by October 1917, and was able to detect aircraft sounds at up to fifteen miles.

The first German bombing raid of 1918 was

Gotha GIV bombers took part in most of the night attacks on London. (Philip Jarrett)

Gotha GIIIs parked in front of a Zeppelin shed, probably at Berchem Ste Agathe in Belgium. (Philip Jarrett)

mounted on the night of 28/29 January, when thirteen Gothas and two Giants were despatched to attack London. In the event seven Gothas and one Giant succeeded in doing so, killing sixty-seven civilians, injuring another 166, and causing damage of nearly £190,000. The raid was thwarted to some degree by fog, as far as the Gothas were concerned, while one of the Giants had engine trouble and was forced to turn back, having jettisoned its bombs into the sea off Ostende.

Crossing the English coast at intervals from 20.00 between Harwich and the North Foreland, three Gothas bombed London and the remaining four attacked Ramsgate, Margate, Sheerness and Sandwich. The Giant also reached London just after midnight, and one of its 660 lb bombs caused the worst single bombing incident of the war when it hit the Odhams Press building in Long Acre, killing thirty-eight people and injuring eighty-five.

One of the Gothas involved in the London attack dropped its bombs on Hampstead at 21.45 and was then tracked by searchlights as it flew over northeast London. The beams attracted the attention of two patrolling Sopwith Camel pilots of No 44 Squadron from Hainault – Captain George Hackwill and Lieutenant Charles Banks – who at once gave chase and independently picked up the glow from the Gotha's exhausts as it passed over Romford at 10,000 feet. Banks was flying a Camel with an unconventional armament; in addition to

its normal pair of Vickers guns it also carried a Lewis, mounted on the upper wing centre section and using the new RTS ammunition. Designed by Richard Threlfall and Son, this combined explosive and incendiary qualities.

It was Banks who attacked first, closing from the left to about thirty yards behind the Gotha and opening fire with all three guns. Hackwill meanwhile closed in from the right and also opened fire, effectively boxing in the German bomber and presenting an impossible situation to its gunner, whose field of fire was restricted. After ten minutes or so the Gotha caught fire and dived into the ground near Wickford, where it exploded. It would almost certainly have crashed anyway, even if it had not caught fire, for a subsequent examination of the crew's bodies revealed that the pilot had been shot through the neck. Hackwill and Banks were each awarded the Military Cross for their exploit. Other Gothas were also attacked that night, briefly and without result, by pilots of Nos 39, 50, 61 and 78 Squadrons RFC, and by a Sopwith 1½-Strutter of the RNAS from Dover.

An hour after the last Gotha had cleared the coast, the *Riesenflugzeug* was over Sudbury, having made landfall over Hollesley Bay, east of Ipswich, and was approaching London via a somewhat tortuous route. By this time, at least forty-four fighters were searching for it. It was sighted by two of them, from an unidentified squadron, not long after

The Gotha GV entered service in August 1917. Some 36 aircraft of this type were involved in night attacks on England. (Philip Jarrett)

crossing the coast, but they lost contact with it and it was next sighted by the crew of a No 39 Squadron Bristol fighter at about 23.00 near Harlow. The pilot of the Bristol, Lieutenant John Goodyear, positioned himself behind the Giant and fired a long burst from his Vickers, but was then hurled aside by the slipstream; this Giant, an R12, was fitted with six coupled engines driving three propellers, and the wash they created was enormous.

He tried again, and the same thing happened. On the third attempt, with the Bristol now running through heavy defensive fire, he attempted to position underneath the Giant so that his gunner, 1st Air Mechanic W.T. Merchant, could bring fire from his Lewis gun to bear. At that moment a burst of fire from one of the German gunners shattered the Bristol's petrol tank and wounded Merchant slightly in the arm. A few moments later the engine stopped and Goodyear glided down to make a faultless engine-off landing at North Weald, whose flarepath he had seen in the distance.

Shortly after it had released its bombs over London, the Giant was picked up east of Woolwich by a Sopwith Camel of No 44 Squadron flown by Lieutenant Bob Hall, a South African. Hall followed it as far as Foulness, cursing in helpless frustration all the way because he could not get his guns to work. The Giant got away.

The anti-aircraft barrage scored one success that night, but unfortunately its victim was a Camel of No 78 Squadron flown by Lieutenant Idris Davies, whose engine was stopped by a near shell burst at 11,000 feet over Woolwich. Davies tried to glide back to Sutton's Farm, but he hit telegraph wires near the Hornchurch signal box and was catapulted out of the cockpit. He fell between the railway lines, amazingly without injury, but the Camel was a complete loss. Forty minutes later Davies was sitting in another Camel, ready to take off if need be. Mostly, the anti-aircraft gunners co-operated very well with the RFC, and held their fire when friendly fighters were known to be overhead.

The following night witnessed the most remarkable night battle of the war, when three Giants out of four despatched, attacked southern England. The fourth, having developed engine trouble over the Channel, bombed fortifications near Gravelines before returning to its base, while the others crossed the English coast between Southend and the Naze. One of these, the R26, developed engine trouble soon after crossing the coast and began losing height, so its crew jettisoned the bomb load and limped back across the Channel on two engines, eventually landing at Ostende.

A second Giant, the R39, came inland via the Blackwater estuary just after 22.00, and ten minutes later it was sighted by Captain Arthur Dennis of No 37 Squadron, who was flying a BE12b. The latter, developed from the older BE2c, had enjoyed some success in the night fighting role, one of No 37 Squadron's aircraft having shot down Zeppelin L48 in June 1917. It was armed with a single Lewis gun, mounted on the port side of the cockpit and synchronised to fire through the propeller. Dennis

Sopwith Camel F1 B3834, oddly named Wonga Bonga *and based with the RNAS at Manston, was twice in action against Gothas. It shared in the destruction of an enemy bomber on 22 August 1917, flown by Flt Lt A.F. Brandon.* (Philip Jarrett)

opened fire from close range, braving fire from two of the Giant's machine-guns, and scored hits on the bomber's fuselage before drawing off to change his ammunition drum. On the second approach, however, he was buffeted by the Giant's slipstream, and on recovery found that he had lost contact with the target.

The R39 approached London from the

Crews of No 141 (Home Defence) Squadron at Biggin Hill, Kent, with their Bristol F2b Fighters in 1918. (Philip Jarrett)

Bristol F2b C4814 'D' of No 11 Squadron (Philip Jarrett)

north-west at approximately 11,000 feet and was next sighted by Bob Hall of No 44 Squadron, who pursued it until it became lost in the haze near Roehampton. Once again, Hall's guns gave trouble and he had no opportunity to open fire. Meanwhile, the Giant had dropped its bombs on residential areas between Acton and Richmond Park, the crew having apparently mistaken Hammersmith Bridge for Tower Bridge, which was several miles to the east. South of the Thames, the R39 was attacked briefly and with no visible result by Captain F.L. Luxmoore of No 78 Squadron, flying a Sopwith Camel. He fired fifty rounds on his first pass, but as he made a second firing run one of his bullets struck the Camel's propeller and the brilliant tracer element flew back into his face, temporarily blinding him. By the time his night vision was restored, the bomber had vanished.

Shortly after this the R39, now down to 9,500 feet and travelling very fast, was located by Captain G.H. Hackwill of No 44 Squadron, who was also flying a Camel. Hackwill gave chase and fired 600 rounds from long range before shortage of fuel compelled him to break off. The Giant was last seen as it crossed the coast near Hythe by 2nd Lieutenants F.V. Bryant and V.H. Newton, the crew of an Armstrong Whitworth FK8 of No 50 Squadron. They too gave chase, but lost the bomber in haze.

The third Giant, the R25, crossed the coast near Foulness at 10.50 pm and was almost immediately attacked by 2nd Lieutenant F.R. Kitton of No 37 Squadron, flying a BE2e. Diving his aircraft at a shuddering 100 mph, he got under the Giant's tail and fired a complete drum of ammunition at it, observing several hits, but lost the bomber while he was busy rearming. The R25 was next attacked by Bob Hall of No 44 Squadron at 23.15 over Benfleet, but his guns kept on jamming as he pursued it. He was joined by 2nd Lieutenant H.A. Edwardes, also of No 44 Squadron, who fired three long bursts before his guns also jammed.

By this time the R25 was taking violent evasive action. The battle had now attracted three more Camels, all from No 44 Squadron; the first on the scene was 2nd Lieutenant T.M. O'Neill, who fired 300 rounds before his guns jammed too. Next came the squadron commander, Major Murlis Green, who was flying a Camel equipped with two Lewis guns using RTS ammunition. He had already made one run, only to break away when he almost flew into O'Neill's fire. Now he closed in again to be greeted by the full attention of the Giant's rear gunner. Undeterred, he fired three-quarters of a drum at the bomber before suffering a stoppage which he was unable to clear. As his second Lewis also refused to function, he had no choice but to return to base to have the trouble put right.

Bristol F2bs of No 141 Squadron at Biggin Hill, late 1918. (Philip Jarrett)

Major G.W. Murlis Green, DSO, MC, OC No 44 Squadron, taking off from Hainault Farm, Essex, in a Sopwith Camel modified for night fighting. Note the machine-guns mounted above the upper wing – a special night fighting modification. (Philip Jarrett)

The R25 was now in trouble. The Camels' fire had put one of its engines out of action and some of its instruments had also been smashed. Although unable to maintain height with a full bomb load, and with their speed down to about 60 mph, the crew decided to press on to London. The Giant's bombs fell in open ground near Wanstead. Up to this point the R25 had been harried by Bob Hall, who was able to fire only five rounds before each stoppage; he now lost his target, but encountered the R39 a few miles to the west.

The R25 scraped home to Ostende, having survived successive attacks by five fighters. They had collectively fired over 800 rounds at her, and after landing she was found to have taken no fewer than eighty-eight hits. Had the fighters not suffered continual gun stoppages, there seems little doubt that they would have brought down the bomber. 23

This photograph of Sopwith Camel F1 of No 44 Squadron clearly shows the night fighting modifications. The pilot is thought to be Capt G.H. Hackwill. (Philip Jarrett)

Sopwith Camel, unit unidentified, in night fighting colours. Note the fuselage artwork. (Philip Jarrett)

Several armament installations, this one included, were tried out on the Sopwith 1½-Strutter. Something of a 'do-it-yourself' night fighter, the modified aircraft were known as Sopwith 'Comics' by their crews. (Philip Jarrett)

However, there were other factors in their failure to do so; analysing the action later, the Camel pilots of No 44 Squadron realised that the Giant's sheer size had led them to believe that they had been firing from a much closer range than was actually the case. Instead of closing to within 50 yards, as they had thought at the time, they must have been anything up to 250 yards away.

The last German aircraft raid on Britain in World War I took place on the night of 20/21 May 1918. Twenty-eight Gothas and three Giants set out to attack London, and were met by a vastly more effective night fighter force than had been the case four months earlier, at the time of the previous night raids. Seventy-four Camels and SE5s went up to intercept the bombers, shooting down three Gothas, while the anti-aircraft defences claimed two more and a sixth crashed in Essex after engine failure. It was the biggest loss suffered by the German bombers in a single night's operations over England, and it was to be more than two decades before they came again.

The cessation of attacks on England by heavier-than-air machines meant that fighters could be released for service in the night fighting role on the Western Front, and on 12 June 1918 No 151 Squadron formed for this purpose at Hainault Farm, combining one flight each from Nos 44, 78 and 112 Squadrons. The first flight of Camels crossed the Channel on 16 June; by the 26th the whole squadron was installed at Famechon, moving to Fontaine-sur-Maye on 2 July. Its first success was achieved by Captain A.B. Yuille, who sighted and attacked a Gotha in the early hours of 25 July. The

Gotha crash-landed behind the British lines with both engines out of action and its observer wounded. In the months that followed, No 151 Squadron was to carry out many night interceptions, as well as mounting night intruder operations against the German bomber airfields, and by the end of the war its pilots had claimed the destruction of twenty-six enemy aircraft. It was to remain a night fighter unit for most of its career, and the last aircraft it used in this role in the late 1950s was the potent Gloster Javelin – a far cry from the Camels with which it pioneered its night fighting techniques.

On 8 August, 1918 – a date later described by the German commander, Field Marshal Ludendorff in his memoirs as 'the black day of the German Army' – the First French Army under *Général* Debeney and General Rawlinson's Fourth British Army attacked on a fifteen-mile front east of Amiens. By 15.00 the Allied forces had made advances of up to seven miles and taken 7,000 prisoners; the offensive was supported by 430 tanks, the whole of the British Tank Corps less one brigade.

During the week preceding the offensive, the Allied air forces made numerous attacks on enemy airfields, notably those occupied by the *Schlachtstaffeln*, the German ground attack squadrons. In the early hours of 5 August, two Camels of No 151 Squadron, flown by Captain S. Cockerell and Captain W.H. Haynes, carried out intruder patrols over Estrées and Guizancourt aerodromes; Cockerell arrived over Estrées just as enemy aircraft were landing and dropped a bomb, which burst about fifty yards from it, and then

Top and above: *The Airco DH4, seen in these two photographs, made an excellent night fighter. It has been called the 'Mosquito' of WWI.*
(Philip Jarrett)

turned and fired 200 rounds at it from close range. At that moment all the lights went out and Cockerell was unable to see any result, so he dropped two more bombs in the hope of hitting something before returning to base. Shortly afterwards Haynes also appeared over Estrées, having found nothing worthwhile at the other airfield, and attacked one of three Gothas which he saw approaching. The Gotha took evasive action and he lost it. He dropped his bombs on a searchlight battery and then also headed for home, his guns having jammed.

On the next night, two Camels of No 151 Squadron again visited Estrées and Guizancourt. The first to arrive was Major C.J.Q. Brand, who dropped two bombs on the hangars at Guizancourt and then attacked a large two-seater which was coming in to land. He attacked it again on the ground, but broke off when all the lights went out. He remained in the vicinity of the airfield for the next half hour, dropping two bombs in the path of an aircraft which was about to touch down, then strafed the hangars and searchlights. Shortly after-

wards he attacked another enemy aircraft, but was himself attacked from the rear by a German scout and returned to base. In the 1939–45 war, this officer – then Air Vice-Marshal Sir Quintin Brand, DSO, MC, DFC – was to command No 10 Group, RAF Fighter Command, in the Battle of Britain. The other Camel of No 151 Squadron that night was flown by Captain Cockerell, who dropped four bombs on the hangars at Guizancourt and then shot up four searchlights until they went out. Soon afterwards he attacked a Gotha, which crash-landed some distance from the airfield.

It was on this night – 6/7 August, 1918 – that the German Naval Airship Division mounted its last raid on the British isles. Four airships were involved; they were the L53, L56, L65 and L70, and the latter was shot down in flames by a DH4 from Great Yarmouth NAS, crewed by Major Egbert Cadbury and Captain Robert Leckie. It fell into the sea near King's Lynn, Norfolk. The great irony was that among the twenty-two dead was the man who had been the original architect of the night offensive against Britain, Peter Strasser.

CHAPTER TWO

THE COMPLACENT YEARS, 1919–39

By the time the Armistice was concluded in November 1918, Britain's night air defences had reached a remarkable degree of sophistication. There were sixteen home defence squadrons under the command of No 6 Brigade, RAF, together with nine night training squadrons, with a total strength of 355 aircraft. Of these, 145 were Sopwith Camels and fifty-five Bristol Fighters; the remainder comprised eighty-two Avro 504s, sixty FE2bs/ds and thirteen BE12s.

By this time, air fighting tactics were well thought out, as was illustrated in a paper written by Murlis Green (who retired as a Group Captain, and whose name became hyphenated somewhere *en route*) in the early 1920s for the RAF Staff College.

'On a dark night with no moon the exhaust flames of a stationary engine machine will usually be seen before the outline of the machine itself, but on a clear moonlight night the outline of the machine is generally first seen.

'After patrolling for an hour or so in the dark without seeing anything there is a tendency, when a hostile machine is at last seen, to drive straight at it firing both guns. This method seldom leads to success as the flash of the machine-guns, even when shielded, usually impairs the pilot's sight to such an extent that after the first few rounds have been fired he loses the target.

'The method found most successful up to now is as follows. Once you have seen your objective you must not take your eyes off him until he is destroyed or you wish to break off the fight. Turn your machine quickly into the same direction as he is going and get behind and slightly below him. If you have a 45 degree mounting use it. If your guns fire in line of flight close up until almost colliding, throttle back and open fire.

'There are two reasons why it is important not to open fire until extremely close range has been reached. Firstly, it is difficult to distinguish friend from foe at night, as of course crosses cannot be distinguished from circles, so that one has to rely entirely on silhouettes. Secondly, range is very deceptive at night.'

Murlis Green was a firm advocate of upward-firing guns mounted at an angle of 45 degrees, and postulated a twin-engined night fighter armed with .5 in machine-guns in this configuration; but it was to be twenty years before the concept was adopted operationally, and then by the Germans, who used it with devastating effect against the RAF's night bombers.

From the summer of 1917, the RFC had used wireless telegraphy (W/T) in the fight against the German raiders. BE12s of Nos 37 and 50 Squadrons, operating in pairs and equipped with continuous-wave transmitters, patrolled north and south of the Thames and reported, by means of coded signals in Morse, the movements of incoming enemy aircraft to ground stations at Wormwood Scrubs and the Hotel Cecil in the Strand, London.

But the most significant development was radio telephony (R/T). Experimental work in this field was centralised at Biggin Hill early in 1917, and after successful trials the Bristol Fighters of No 141 Squadron were fitted with air-ground R/T sets in January 1918. Shortly afterwards, the principal airfields in the London Air Defence Area (LADA) were equipped with short-range transmitters so that they could communicate directly with their own squadron aircraft; in these early days, although all aircraft carried receivers, only those of the flight commanders were equipped to transmit. All the LADA squadrons were equipped with R/T by the end of August 1918, squadrons and their bases both being allocated callsigns. The collective callsign for all No 6 Brigade aircraft was Menagerie, and the other allocated callsigns were as follows:

Squadron	Base	Aircraft
37	Yukon	Husky
39	Bona	Buffalo
44	Niger	Hippo
50	Bark	Dingo
61	Rockies	Grizzly
78	Cub	Lion
112	Darling	Duckbill
141	Dollars	Rhino
143	Pouch	Kangaroo

Patrol areas were given geographical designations,

such as Brazil, Canada and Mexico, while other code words were used to precede orders transmitted from the ground. For example, Gulls meant the two highest aircraft on patrol, Penguins meant all other aircraft, and Rum signified recall. An aircraft forced to abandon its patrol transmitted the code-word Blanket. Height alterations were expressed in thousands of feet: 'Step up one' meant climb 1,000 feet, while 'Step down two' was the order to descend 2,000 feet.

The introduction of R/T led to vast improvements in the LADA control and reporting system. A central operations room was set up at Spring Gardens, near Admiralty Arch in London, and was declared operational on 12 September 1918. It was equipped with a large plotting table covered with a squared map of the London area and overlooked by a dais from which LADA's commander and subordinate officers could overlook the proceedings. The ten plotters received information through telephone head-sets from twenty-six sub-control centres, which in turn received their information from gun and searchlight sights, sound locators and observation posts, and transferred it to the map, using a disc to indicate single enemy aircraft and a rectangle to indicate a formation, with arrows denoting courses. During a major raid, coloured indicators were used to differentiate between enemy formations. Defending fighters were represented by aircraft-shaped counters. The commander of the London Air Defence Area, Major-General E.B. Ashmore, could break into the plotters' telephone lines if he needed further information, while Brigadier-General T.C.R. Higgins, GOC No 6 Brigade, had direct lines to his fighter wings.

In its definitive form, the new control and reporting system was installed too late to have a decisive impact on the air defence of Great Britain, for by September 1918 enemy air raids had ceased. But it was the foundation of a greatly enhanced and refined system which, with the priceless gift of radar, was to be the salvation of the nation in 1940, and which was ultimately to provide fighters with the eyes that would enable them to locate and destroy enemy bombers at night.

The four years of World War I marked an incredible leap forward in the embryonic science of military aviation – especially in Britain, which had progressed from aircraft that could barely fly across the Channel in 1914 to a strategic bomber (the Handley Page V/1500) that was preparing to bomb Berlin from East Anglia in 1918. Yet, almost before the guns had ceased firing, the British Admiralty and the War Office joined forces in a determined bid to abolish the Royal Air Force – the service in which technical advance was most apparent – as a separate organisation.

One man – the Chief of the Air Staff, Air Chief Marshal Sir Hugh Trenchard – was equally as determined that the RAF should retain its separate identity, but drastic cuts in post-war defence expenditure made his task a formidable one. By the end of 1921 the strength of the RAF was at a very low ebb; apart from training establishments, there were only five squadrons based in the United Kingdom, and only one of these (No 25) was a fighter squadron. Yet this was a mere three years after the government had published statistics showing that in four years of war, Zeppelins and German bombers between them had killed or injured over 4,000 British civilians, mostly during night raids.

The parlous state of Britain's air defences was highlighted by an article in *The Times* in March 1922, which alerted the British public to the fact that the French Air Force, far from dismantling its assets wholesale, possessed a front-line combat force of 300 bombers and 300 fighters. The shock was profound, especially as relations between Britain and her former ally were poor at this time; the Air Staff, carrying out an assessment of the probable damage such a bomber force might do, and basing it on the results of the Gotha raids, calculated that the French had the capability to kill 1,700 people and injure 3,300 in London in the first twenty-four hours of an air attack, followed by 1,275 killed and 2,475 injured in the second twenty-four hours, and 850 killed and 1,650 injured in every subsequent twenty-four hours. In other words, the French bombers would theoretically be able to kill and injure, in only three days, twice the number of casualties inflicted on British civilians during the whole of the war.

Within a month a defence sub-committee recommended that the strength of the RAF be greatly increased, and the Cabinet gave its approval to the formation of twenty new squadrons for home defence. In 1923 this was further increased to a recommended fifty-two squadrons, totalling 600 aircraft. It was not before time; in the spring of 1923 there was still only one fighter squadron, No 56, in the whole of the United Kingdom (the other, No 43, was on detachment to Turkey). Yet no thought was given to the formation of specialist night fighter squadrons, even though the French, armed with the excellent Breguet XIV, had shown considerable expertise in night bombing operations during the war.

Re-equipment proceeded at a relatively slow pace, the fighter squadrons standardising on the Sopwith Snipe, the RAF's most modern fighter when the war ended. A decade later, the biplane fighters with which the RAF's home defence squadrons were armed were not much further advanced, and although a new generation of monoplane fighters was on the horizon the prototypes, in

The magnificent Breguet XIV, seen here in civilian markings post-war, pioneered French night bombing techniques in WWI. (Author)

The Sopwith Snipe was the RAF's most modern fighter in the years immediately after WWI. This rare photograph shows Snipes in South
Russia, 1919. (Author)

RAF pilots occasionally took to the night skies in biplane fighters such as the Bristol Bulldog . . .

. . . But day flying was hazardous enough, as this photograph of an upturned Armstrong Whitworth Siskin shows. (Both Author)

1934, had yet to fly.

On the technical front, however, decisions were being taken that would have far-reaching importance, particularly in the context of night fighter development. In 1934 A.P. Rowe of the Directorate of Scientific Research in the Air Ministry, seriously alarmed by the state of Britain's air defences, informed his Director, H.E. Wimperis, that unless

science were applied to air fighting Britain would certainly lose any war fought within the next ten years. Wimperis was impressed by the argument, and proposed to the Secretary of State, Lord Londonderry, that a scientific committee should be formed within the Air Ministry to survey air defence. He further suggested that the chairman of this committee should be H.T. Tizard, a former

Royal Flying Corps pilot who was now Chairman of the Aeronautical Research Committee.

In 1935 one of the first matters to come before Tizard's committee was the so-called 'death ray', much beloved by science fiction writers, which had been proposed by various 'inventors' since the 1914-18 war. Tizard might have dismissed the concept out of hand; instead, he consulted on its possibilities with R.A. Watson-Watt, Superintendent of the Radio Department of the National Physical Laboratory. Watson-Watt and his staff buried the 'death ray' notion once and for all, but Watson-Watt recalled something odd. In 1932, the Post Office had reported that aircraft sometimes interfered with radio signals and re-radiated them. What if, Watson-Watt thought, a ground station transmitted a radio pulse which would be reflected back by an aircraft and picked up by the ground station?

One of Watson-Watt's staff, A.F. Wilkins, made further calculations, and as a result Watson-Watt submitted an historic document to the Air Ministry on 12 February, 1935. Its title was *Detection and Location of Aircraft by Radio Methods*. It was to change the course of air warfare.

While Watson-Watt and his team proceeded with their early experiments into what would even-

tually become known as radar, the Air Staff had been turning its attention to the concept of a two-seat fighter suitable for both day and night operations, and in April 1935 Specification F9/35 was issued. Most of the major British aircraft constructors – Armstrong Whitworth, Boulton Paul, Bristol, Fairey, Hawker and Supermarine – submitted tenders, and in the end the choice was narrowed down to two proposals, those put forward by Hawker and Boulton Paul. (A contract was also drawn up around the Fairey submission, but this never went beyond the design stage).

Construction of the Hawker proposal, the Hotspur – basically a Hawker Henley with the addition of a power-operated gun turret – was delayed by Hawker's preoccupation with Hurricane production, and the sole prototype did not fly until 14 June 1938. In the meantime, in March 1937, Boulton Paul had received a contract for eighty-seven production examples of its design, the P82, to Specification F5/37, and the name Defiant was adopted. The full programme of flight trials was completed at the Aeroplane and Armament Experimental Establishment (A&AEE) at Martlesham Heath in February 1938, the prototype flying without its four-gun turret.

The turret, known as the Boulton Paul A Mk IID,

The Boulton Paul Defiant was a disaster as a day fighter, but adapted very well to the night fighting role. This example, N1751, served with No 256 Squadron in the winter of 1940–41. (Philip Jarrett)

The AI-equipped Bristol Blenheim 1F gave the RAF a limited night fighting capability. This example is seen bearing the code markings of the night fighter OTU, No 54. (Philip Jarrett)

was installed in the second prototype Defiant (K8620) which flew with a Rolls-Royce Merlin II engine on 18 May 1938. The first production Defiant I flew on 30 July that year. Fifty Defiants of the first production batch had been completed by the end of 1939, and the first Defiant squadron, No 264, began to rearm with the new type at Martlesham Heath on 8 December.

But the Defiant, at this stage, was not regarded as anything other than a day fighter; its part in the air war at night was to come much later, as we shall see.

In 1938, the Air Staff had identified a requirement for a long-range escort fighter, and this led to the conversion of a number of Blenheim Mk I bombers to the fighter role under the designation Mk IF. To convert the aircraft to a fighter proved relatively simple, by adding a self-contained battery of four forward-firing Browning machine-guns in a shallow pack fitting flush under the bomb bay. The first squadron to rearm with the Blenheim IF, in

September 1938, was No 600 at Hendon, and four others (Nos 23, 25, 29 and 604) had re-equipped by the end of the year. By the outbreak of war in September 1939 Nos 64 and 601 Squadrons had also rearmed with the type.

By the spring of 1940 it was becoming obvious that the Blenheim IF, allied with the still experimental airborne interception (AI) radar, was the only aircraft on the RAF's inventory capable of filling the night fighter gap, and on 18 April 1940 the Fighter Interception Unit was formed at Tangmere under the command of Wing Commander Peter Chamberlain, six Blenheims being allocated for operational trials with the AI Mk III.

Ten days earlier, the Germans had invaded Norway, and on 10 May 1940 their armies struck in France and the Low Countries. All the resources of Fighter Command would soon be put to the test.

CHAPTER THREE

NIGHT FIGHTERS IN THE BATTLE OF FRANCE

France's ANF les Mureaux 113 and 115 general purpose aircraft were used to develop night fighting tactics in the years before WWII. (ECP Armées)

When war broke out on 3 September, 1939, the only belligerent nation to have a dedicated night fighter unit on its order of battle was France. The French Air Ministry had been conscious of the need for air defence at night since 1934, and at the beginning of 1939 the night defence role was assigned to two *Groupes de Chasse de Nuit*, GCN 3/1 at Etampes and GCN 2/4 at Reims. Both were equipped with Mureaux 113 two-seat general purpose aircraft, GCN

GCN 2/4, the French Air Force pre-war night fighter unit, also operated a few Dewoitine D500s (seen here) and D501s. (ECP Armées)

2/4 also having an *escadrille* (flight) of Dewoitine D501 single-seat fighters. All these units had been assigned to other duties by the outbreak of war.

On 25 February 1939 another night fighter unit, the newly-formed GCN 1/13, took delivery of its first three twin-engined Potez 630 fighters at Reims. This aircraft was the result of a French Air Ministry specification, dated 31 October 1934, for a light multi-seat air defence fighter capable of night missions. Series production began at the beginning of 1939, and during the following year the 13e *Escadre de Chasse de Nuit*'s two groups, 1/13 and 2/13, progressively rearmed with a derivative, the Potez 631. This aircraft, powered by two Gnome-Rhône radial engines, had evolved from a 1934 specification for a three-seat strategic fighter; armed with two 20 mm cannon and two 7.5 mm machine-guns, it had an operational ceiling of 31,000 feet and a maximum speed of 275 mph at 14,800 feet.

From 22 September 1939, GCN 1/13 sent detachments to Melun-Villaroche for operational training, its pilots practising night interception techniques with the aid of searchlights on the ground. On 1 January 1940 both groups split up into four independent *escadrilles*, and on 10 May 1940 the order of battle was as follows:

Unit	Establishment (Aircraft)	Available	Base
ECN 1/13	12	8	Meaux-Villenoy
ENC 2/13	11	7	Melun-Villaroche
ECN 3/13	12	10	Le Plessis
ECN 4/13	12	7	Betz-Boulliancy
ECN 5/13	11	11	Loyettes

ECN 4/13, in fact, was seriously under strength, three of its crews having been sent to reinforce 2/13 and two more to reinforce 1/13. All flights stood alert from 10 to 16 May, but there were no night interceptions of enemy aircraft.

On 17 May 1940, ten days after the German assault in the west began, *Armée de l'Air* HQ – aware that the night fighter force possessed over forty serviceable aircraft that could usefully be employed elsewhere – decided to use them in the assault role. Accordingly, later that day eighteen Potez of ECN 1/13, 2/13 and 4/13 took off from their bases in the Paris area to attack enemy motorised columns near Fourmies.

It was a costly venture. Of the six Potez 631s of

The Potez 631 was of the same lineage as the Potez 63 reconnaissance aircraft, seen here, but had a redesigned 'solid' nose and a lengthened cockpit reminiscent of the Messerschmitt 110's – an aircraft for which it was often mistaken. (ECP Armées)

2/13, only two regained their base at Melun. Of the others, *Lieutenant* Guillier crash-landed near Montceaux; *Adjudant* Delmotte managed to land at Chantilly-les-Aigles, wounded and with his aircraft shot to ribbons, *Sous-Lieutenant* Reyter made a forced landing at Laon with his port engine out of action, and the *Groupe*'s commander, *Capitaine* Petit de Mirbeck, was shot down in flames over the enemy lines. One of the four aircraft of 4/13 was hit and crash-landed at Cambrai with its pilot wounded; the gunner of a second was killed by a flak shell. The eight Potez of 1/13 returned to Meaux, but all were damaged.

The night fighter *escadrilles* scored their first victory on 18 May – during the daytime. At 14.00 three Potez of 1/13 flown by *Capitaine* Treilland, *Sergent-Chef* Post and *Adjudant* Guichard attacked a lone Heinkel 111 and forced it down north of Braine. That same afternoon, *Capitaine* Pierre Pouyade (who was later to rise to fame as commander of the *Regiment Normandie-Niemen*, the Free French air unit that fought on the Russian front), together with *Adjudants* Martin and Delage – all of 4/13 – intercepted a formation of ten He 111s and Me 110s over Creil. Two of the bombers were hit and damaged, but Delage was himself hit and had to make an emergency landing at Beauvais. On the way home, *Adjudant* Martin was successively attacked and hit by a He 111, a Me 110, French anti-aircraft fire and an errant Morane 406; he nevertheless managed to reach base safely.

On the morning of 19 May, six He 111s were intercepted by *Sous-Lieutenant* Merle, *Adjudant* Guichard and *Sergent-Chef* Post of 1/13. The French pilots made their attack through heavy friendly anti-aircraft fire, loosing off hundreds of rounds into a Heinkel that was lagging behind the rest. The bomber crash-landed near Braine with one engine in flames. In the early evening, *Adjudant-Chef* Chambrias, *Adjudant* Guichard and *Sergent-Chef* Post engaged six more Heinkels at high altitude. A Heinkel was set on fire and began to lose height steadily, streaming smoke, but at that point the French pilots were forced to break off the action through lack of fuel and the bomber was not seen to crash.

The Potez 631s of 2/13 also exchanged shots with a Dornier 17 in the evening of the 19th, but no result was observed. The following evening two aircraft of 2/13 were attacked by six Dewoitine 520s, which severely damaged one of the Potez before they realised their error. One could not blame the French fighter pilots; with its long cockpit canopy and twin fins the Potez 631 bore a strong resemblance to the Messerschmitt 110 when viewed from certain angles.

At 10.55 am on 21 May, *Sous-Lieutenant* Boursain and *Sergent-Chef* Post of 2/13 joined forces with a pair of Bloch 152s of GCN 2/1 and 2/9 in an attack on a Dornier 17. The four fighters each made two passes and shot the bomber down in flames in the forest of Halate, near Creil. That same day, the

Bloch MB152 fighters, seen here in Vichy markings, equipped France's local defence flights in the summer of 1940, operating in both the day and night role. They enjoyed some success in the former, but none at all in the latter. (ECP Armées)

problem of misidentification cropped up again with tragic consequences when two Potez of 4/13 were again attacked by D520s of GCN 2/3. The Dewoitines made five passes and the Potez were obliged to open fire to defend themselves. A D520 was hit and crashed in the forest of Chantilly, killing the pilot, *Sous-Lieutenant* d'Harcourt. Two days later, a Potez of 1/13 was attacked by Bloch 152s and crash-landed, seriously injuring the pilot. On 24 May, in an attempt to avoid further tragedies of this kind, several Potez 631s were sent on a tour of the fighter bases in the area so that the single-seater pilots could have a good look at them; they were also furnished with larger roundels and a white band was painted along their fuselage sides.

On 25 May the *Luftwaffe* made a series of heavy attacks on the airfields occupied by the night fighter *escadrilles*. At Le Plessis, a Potez 631 of 3/13 was destroyed on the ground and five others damaged. ECN 1/13, whose base at Meaux was badly hit, was transferred to Trilbardou and later to Moissy-Cramayel.

On 27 May, a Potez of 4/13 flown by *Adjudant* Guichard was attacked by seven Me 109s over the front line. Severely wounded, Guichard made a forced landing in enemy-held territory and the 109s continued to strafe the wreck of his aircraft on the ground. Guichard lingered on in hospital for more than a month before succumbing to his injuries on 18 June. On 28 May, 4/13 became the first night fighter unit to receive a modified version of the Potez 631 with heavier armament consisting of four additional machine-guns mounted under the wings. These modifications had been under way since

April, but they took six weeks to complete and in fact only a few machines were to be delivered before the final collapse.

The first day of June saw the operational debut of ECN 5/13, which was assigned to the defence of the Lyon–Saint Etienne–Le Creusot sector. Three of the unit's Potez 631s attacked nine He 111s over Vienne and damaged one of them, but the three Potez were also damaged and one crew member wounded. The next day 5/13 took part in two more battles; at 08.00 hours two Potez 631s attacked nine Heinkels over Lyon, but they were forced to break off when they themselves were attacked by four Me 110s. At 16.00, the same two French pilots – *Capitaine* Perdrizet and *Sergent* Farriol – attacked a formation of thirty-five He 111s at 25,000 feet over Vienne. Farriol chased a straggling Heinkel for over sixty miles, firing off all his ammunition at it, and the enemy bomber limped away, trailing a stream of smoke.

Also on 2 June, ECN 4/13 had yet another brush with friendly forces when *Capitaine* Pouyade and *Adjudant* Martin were fired on by a French anti-aircraft battery while on patrol over Villers-Cotterets. Pouyade, his aircraft in flames, made a wheels-up landing and escaped from the wreck with slight burns. His observer, however, was severely burned and his gunner wounded. *Adjudant* Martin, who had now been shot at by Frenchmen on three separate occasions and who had collected no fewer than fifteen shell holes in his Potez, stormed into his CO's office on his return and demanded a transfer from the *Armée de l'Air*. His request was turned down.

In another incident that day, *Sergent-Chef* Post of 1/13 was also wounded by friendly shellfire while carrying out an air observation sortie over Lassigny. There seemed to be no end to the peril; on 3 June *Sous-Lieutenant* Merle of 1/13 was attacked in rapid succession by French anti-aircraft fire, seven Me 109s and a Bloch 152; he escaped by the skin of his teeth and pronounced the 109s to be the least dangerous adversaries he had met that day! Two Potez which took off from Melun later in the day to intercept a formation of Heinkels were also given a hot reception by their own base's AA defences on their return, fortunately without damage.

Sous-Lieutenant Biger of ECN 1/13 was lost on 3 June; he was patrolling over Lassigny with *Sous-Lieutenant* Boursain when they were surprised by five Me 109s. Biger went down in flames and Boursain managed to get away. Another Potez, flown by *Lieutenant* Guillier of 2/13, attacked a Dornier 17 and set it on fire, but it disappeared in the haze to the north of the forest of Compiègne.

During the week that followed the night fighter bases were hit repeatedly by the *Luftwaffe* and several Potez 631s were destroyed on the ground. The last air combat took place on 10 June, when *Adjudant* Ravet claimed an Me 109 probably destroyed over Rozay. After that there followed several days of confused withdrawal to the south; by 23 June ECN 1/13, 2/13, 3/13 and 4/13 had pulled back to Nîmes-Garons, while 5/13 was at Marignane.

At 13.00 that day, the four *escadrilles* were ordered to take off and attack armoured columns in the Moirans area. However, a heavy rainfall had turned the grass area into a quagmire and only seven out of fifteen aircraft managed to take off. Six of these attacked the target, and all returned to base.

It was the end. In six weeks of operations the night fighter *escadrilles* had destroyed nine enemy aircraft and claimed thirteen more probably destroyed. Ten Potez 631s had been destroyed through enemy action and three more by friendly aircraft and AA fire, together with three seriously damaged. Not once during those six weeks, although some night sorties had been flown, had the Potez crews had the opportunity to carry out a night interception. Nevertheless, GCN 1/13 deserves its place in history as the first unit of its kind to serve operationally with any air force.

CHAPTER FOUR

THE NIGHT DEFENCE OF BRITAIN, 1940–42

The defeat of France in June 1940 was followed by a growing number of incursions into British airspace by enemy aircraft at night. Many of these raids were intercepted by both day fighters and Blenheim night fighters, the latter having already registered some successes as intruders during the Battle of France. At 00.50 on 19 June, for example, an He 111H-4 of 2/KG54 was shot down into the sea off the Norfolk coast by Flight Lieutenant R.M.B Duke-Woolley in a Blenheim of No 23 Squadron, the German crew being captured; on the same night two Heinkels of 4/KG4 were also destroyed, both at 01.15. The first was shot down off Felixstowe by Flight Lieutenant A.G. Malan in a Spitfire of No 74 Squadron, and the second was shot down jointly by a Spitfire of No 19 Squadron and a Blenheim of No 23 Squadron at Fleam Dyke, Cambridgeshire. Unfortunately, the Spitfire pilot,

Flying Officer Petra, was forced to bale out during the combat after his aircraft was hit, while the Blenheim pilot, Squadron Leader O'Brien, baled out after losing control. Both his crew members were killed.

The third victory of the night was achieved at 02.15 by Flying Officer G.E. Ball of No 19 Squadron, who shot down a Heinkel 111H of 6/KG4 into the sea off Margate.

Three more Heinkels were destroyed in the early hours of 26 June. The first, an He 111P-2 of 3/KG4, was shot down into the sea off Hull by Pilot Officers R.A. Smith and R. Marples at 00.17, while two He 111H-3s of 3/KG26 were shot down by pilots of Nos 602 and 603 Squadrons off the Scottish coast.

Interceptions of this kind were aided by the clear, translucent nature of the summer nights, with their

Fighter Command's main adversary in the night skies of Britain was the Heinkel He 111, seen here under fighter attack during the main daylight phase of the Battle of Britain. (Author)

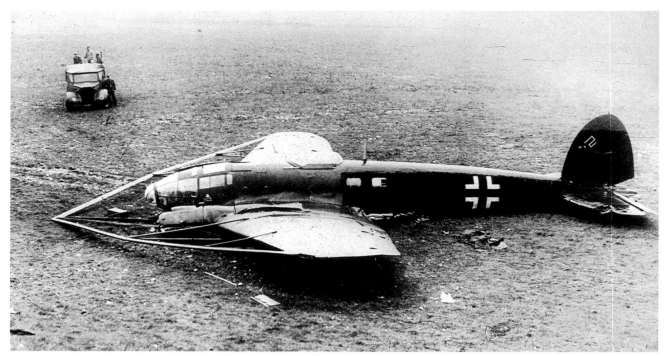

Barrage balloons were always a menace to the German night bombers. This He 111, brought down on British soil, is fitted with a cumbersome balloon 'fender'. (Author)

Blenheim Mk IF, showing AI aerial installation on port wing. (Philip Jarrett)

attendant good visibility. In the following months the *Luftwaffe*'s main effort switched to attacks on coastal shipping. There were still opportunities for the day fighter pilots to make night interceptions, however; at 00.55 on 26 July, for example, an He 111H-4 of 1/KG4 on a mine-laying sortie over the Bristol Channel was shot down by Pilot Officer Cock of No 87 Squadron, flying a Hurricane.

The development of airborne radar in Britain had meanwhile been proceeding well in the summer of 1940, by which time the RAF had five squadrons assigned to night fighting; these were equipped

First line of defence: a Chain Home (CH) radar station on the English coast. (Author)

with Bristol Blenheims and two of them, Nos 29 and 604, were just starting to carry out trials with rudimentary AI Mk III radar. The real pioneering work, however, was undertaken by the Fighter Interception Unit (FIU) at RAF Tangmere, and on the night of 22/23 July 1940 the long-awaited breakthrough came when a radar-equipped Blenheim of this unit intercepted and destroyed a Dornier Do 17 bomber. Flying Officer G. Ashfield, Pilot Officer G.E. Morris and Sergeant R.H. Leyland were patrolling at 10,000 feet when the Chain Home (CH) radar station at Poling established contact with a group of enemy raiders crossing the coast at about 6,000 feet. Information on the enemy's progress was passed to Tangmere Sector Operations Room where the FIU's CO, Wing Commander Peter Chamberlain, was acting as controller. Following Chamberlain's instructions, Ashfield closed on one of the enemy aircraft, the last phase of the interception being controlled by Morris's AI, and at a range of 400 yards identified it as a Do 17 and opened fire. The bomber, of 2/KG3, went down into the sea off the Sussex coast. All four crew members, although wounded, were picked up.

This was the first recorded success of a radar-assisted fighter, and although to some extent it was a lucky interception it showed that the concept was feasible, and the conversion of Blenheims to the night fighter role continued. However, a few squadrons of Blenheims, converted to carry airborne radar, did not provide a solution to the night defence problem; they were too slow, the equipment was very unreliable, and its operators lacked experience. A solution was on the horizon in the shape of the fast, heavily armed Bristol Beaufighter, which was just entering service; but this aircraft was beset by more than the usual crop of teething troubles. In November and December 1940, Beaufighters and radar-equipped Blenheims flew over 600 sorties, made seventy-one radar contacts, and succeeded in destroying only four enemy aircraft.

In an attempt to fill the gap Fighter Command was compelled to adopt what might best be described as desperation measures to counter the enemy night raiders, especially when the *Luftwaffe* began to step up its night offensive against Britain after the failure of its massed daylight attacks in August and September. In the latter month, Air Chief Marshal Sir Hugh Dowding, the AOC-in-C Fighter Command, was ordered by the Air Council to allocate three squadrons of Hawker Hurricanes to night defence, this decision having been taken following the creation of a high-level Night Air Defence Committee earlier in the month. Added to these were three squadrons of Boulton Paul Defiants, which, armed solely with a four-gun power-operated turret, had suffered appalling losses in the day fighter role during the Battle of Britain. During the closing weeks of 1940, these six squadrons of single-engined fighters flew 491 sorties on forty-six nights and destroyed eleven enemy bombers. Operating on a hit-or-miss basis, 41

Boulton Paul Defiant Mk I and crew of No 264 Squadron. (Philip Jarrett)

pilots would seek out enemy bombers trapped in the glare of searchlights and would then go into the attack, risking being shot down by friendly anti-aircraft fire.

One such pilot was Flight Lieutenant Richard Stevens, a Hurricane pilot with No 151 Squadron at RAF Manston. A former civil pilot who had flown the cross-Channel mail route at night and in

Cannon-armed Hurricane IIcs of No 87 Squadron. No 87 was one of the 'specialist' Hurricane-equipped night fighter/intruder squadrons. Its main base was Charmy Down, in Somerset. (Philip Jarrett)

Above and right: *AI Mk IV scanner installation in the nose of a Beaufighter.* (Author)

all weathers, Stevens was thirty years old and a very experienced man by the time he joined No 151 Squadron at the tail-end of the Battle of Britain, in October 1940. At this time the Germans had switched most of their effort to night attacks, and night after night Stevens watched in frustration as the German bombers droned overhead towards the red glare of burning London. He constantly sought permission to try his hand at intercepting the raiders, and at last, one night in December, it was granted.

His early night patrols were disappointing. For several nights running, although the Manston controller assured him that the sky was stiff with enemy bombers, Stevens saw nothing. Then, on the night of 15 January 1941, the shellbursts of the London anti-aircraft defences led him to a Do 17 of 4/KG3, which he chased up to 30,000 feet and then almost down to ground level as the German pilot tried to shake him off. But Stevens hung on, and after two or three short bursts the bomber went down and exploded on the ground.

It was No 151 Squadron's first night victory, and there were more to come. On a second patrol that night, Stevens caught an He 111 of 2/KG53 at 17,000 feet, heading for London, and shot it down into the Thames estuary. Three of the four crew members baled out and were captured. The night's work earned Stevens a Distinguished Flying Cross.

Somehow, it seemed as though Stevens' brace of kills had been a good omen. After that, the RAF's night fighter squadrons appeared to enjoy more success. Men like Flight Lieutenant John Cunningham of No 604 Squadron, now flying fast, heavily-armed Bristol Beaufighters, began to carve out reputations for themselves as bomber destroyers. Cunningham, known by the nickname of 'Cat's Eyes' bestowed on him by the popular press, and which he thoroughly detested, was to destroy no fewer than eight enemy bombers at night in April 1941, having been led expertly to his targets by his AI operator, Sergeant Jimmy Rawnsley. He was to

43

end the war with a score of twenty enemy aircraft destroyed, two probably destroyed and seven damaged, most of them at night. (The 'Cat's Eyes' nickname, of course, was designed to divert attention from the AI radar, which was still highly secret and about which the public as yet knew nothing.)

It was eyesight alone, however, with a little help from searchlights and shellbursts, that brought Richard Stevens to his victims. Shortly after the award of his DFC, he developed ear trouble and was grounded for a while, but he celebrated his return to action on 8 April 1941 by shooting down two He 111s in one night. Two nights later he got another Heinkel and a Ju 88, and a few days later he received a Bar to his DFC. He destroyed yet another Heinkel on the 19th, and on 7 May he accounted for two more. Three nights after that, his claim was one Heinkel destroyed and one probably destroyed. He shot down a further Heinkel on 13 June, damaged one on the 22nd, and on 3 July sent a Ju 88 down in flames. There seemed to be no end to his success; at this time he was the RAF's top-scoring night fighter pilot, enjoying a considerable lead over pilots who flew the radar-equipped Beaufighters.

Stevens experienced a lot of frustration during the summer months of 1941. In June the Germans invaded the Soviet Union, and by the end of July they had withdrawn many of their bomber units from the Western Front. Raids at night over Britain became fewer, and although Stevens continued to fly his lone patrols, for weeks he never saw an enemy bomber. Then, one evening in October, he spotted a Ju 88 slipping inland over the coast of East Anglia and attacked it. The Junkers jettisoned its bombs and turned away, diving low over the water, but Stevens caught it with a burst of fire and sent it into the sea. It was his fourteenth victory.

Soon afterwards, Stevens was posted to another Hurricane unit, No 253 Squadron, as a flight commander, and he immediately set about devising a plan to take the war to the enemy by flying night intruder operations over the German airfields in Holland and Belgium. Later in the war, offensive operations of this kind would become routine, but in December 1941 Stevens was virtually pioneering a new technique. He flew his first night intruder operation on the night of 12/13 December, the day when it was announced that he had been awarded the Distinguished Service Order. He loitered in the vicinity of the bomber airfield at Gilze-Rijen, in Holland, but saw no aircraft and returned home in disappointment.

Three nights later he took off again, heading for the same destination, and never returned. The signal that his squadron commander sent to Group HQ was simple and concise. 'One Hurricane IIc (long-range), 253 Squadron, took off Manston 19.40 on 15 December 1941, to go to Gilze. It has failed to return and is beyond maximum endurance.' It later transpired that he had been shot down either by flak or return fire. He is buried in Bergen-op-Zoom war cemetery in the Netherlands.

The majority of the home-based Hurricane IIc squadrons took part in night intruder operations at one time or another during 1942, and some became specialists in the role. Number 1 Squadron, for example, which was based at RAF Tangmere, destroyed twenty-two enemy aircraft over occupied Europe between 1 April and 1 July that year before moving to Northumberland to convert to Typhoon fighter-bombers, and no fewer than fifteen of these victories were gained by one pilot, Flight Lieutenant Karel Kuttelwascher.

A highly competent and experienced pilot, Kuttelwascher – known by the simpler abbreviation of 'Kut' to his squadron colleagues – had flown with the Czech Air Force for four years before his country was overrun by the Germans, after which he had made his way to Britain via France. He scored his first three kills – all Me 109s – while flying convoy protection and bomber escort missions over the Channel in the spring and early summer of 1941, but it was when No 1 Squadron went over to night intruder operations in April 1942 that Kut really got into his stride. In April 1942 he destroyed three Ju 88s, three Do 217s and an He 111, and on the night of 4/5 May he shot down three He 111s over St André. He destroyed a Do 217 off Dunkirk on 2/3 June, and on the following night he visited St André again to destroy an He 111 and a Do 217, as well as damaging another Dornier.

St André was once again the target on 21/22 June, when Kut shot down a Ju 88 and damaged another. A Do 217 went down before his guns near Trevières on 28/29 June, and his last two victims, also Do 217s, were brought down near Dinard on the night of 1/2 July, when he also damaged a third Dornier. That brought Kut's score to eighteen destroyed, with one probable (an Me 109, his first combat in the RAF, on 2 February 1941) and five damaged. In addition, he may have claimed up to six victories while flying Morane 406 fighters in the Battle of France. After the war, he became a captain with British European Airways, flying Vikings and Elizabethans. He died of a heart attack on 17 August 1959, at the untimely age of 42.

Number 1 Squadron's other leading scorer in the summer of 1942 was the squadron commander, Squadron Leader James MacLachlan, but with five enemy bombers destroyed and three damaged, MacLachlan ws a long way behind his Czech colleague. A remarkable character, 'Mac' had scored six victories in the Battle of Britain and two more

Beaufighter Mk I showing the aerials of the AI Mk IV radar on nose and wings. Note the under-fuselage crew access hatches, which formed windbreaks to facilitate escape, and the 'cheese-grater' flame damping exhaust pipes. (Philip Jarrett)

over Malta, but had himself been shot down and badly wounded in February 1941, losing his left arm above the elbow. He took command of No 1 Squadron in November 1941, having been fitted with an artificial arm in the meantime.

Since the advent of the Bristol Beaufighter, night fighter developments in the RAF had been making steady progress. Delays in the production of AI Mk IV radar equipment had prevented the full complement of five Beaufighter units (Nos 25, 29, 219, 600 and 604 Squadrons) from becoming operational until the spring of 1941, but despite early teething troubles those that were operational had enjoyed some success. The first AI-assisted Beaufighter kill had been claimed on the night of 19/20 November

1940, when Flight Lieutenant John Cunningham and Sgt Phillipson of No 604 Squadron were credited with the destruction of a Ju 88, and by the time all five Beaufighter squadrons reached operational status their efficiency was greatly enhanced by the commissioning of six GCI (Ground Controlled Interception) radar stations on the south and east coasts of England. These could provide fairly wide coverage, and controllers could bring the fighter to within three miles of the target aircraft, at which point the AI Mk IV radar took over. The first GCI-controlled interception was made by John Cunningham on 12 January 1941, but was unsuccessful because the Beaufighter's guns jammed. Then, on 10 May 1941 – the last major

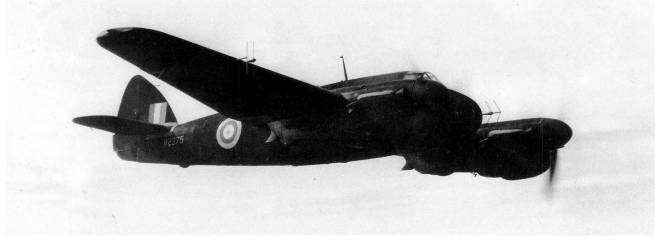

The Merlin-engined Beaufighter Mk II equipped seven RAF night fighter squadrons. (Philip Jarrett)

Boulton Paul Defiant Mk II AA370 with AI aerials. A trials aircraft for much of its career, AA370 went to Karachi in January 1944 and was struck off charge in SEAC in November that year. (Philip Jarrett)

Luftwaffe attack on London – GCI-controlled Beaufighters destroyed fourteen German bombers, the highest loss sustained by the *Luftwaffe* on any one night since the 'Blitz' began.

Thirteen more Beaufighter squadrons were assigned to the night defence of Great Britain in 1941–42, and many of the RAF's night fighter aces scored their early kills while flying the heavy twin-engined fighter. During the closing months of 1941 the *Luftwaffe*'s preoccupation with the eastern front meant that night raids on Britain were sporadic, but in the spring of 1942 the air offensive was renewed with the onset of the so-called 'Baedecker Raids', directed against Britain's historic cities.

Meanwhile, Fighter Command's Defiant night fighter squadrons were being progressively equipped with AI radar. A few Defiants were initially fitted with the AI Mk IV, but from August 1941 the improved Mk VI became available, and Defiants fitted with this set were redesignated Mk IAs. The installation on the Defiant had transmitter and receiver aerials on the wings and the side of the fuselage, the cathode-ray tube display being installed in the pilot's cockpit because there was not enough room in the gun turret. The first unit to be so equipped was No 264 Squadron, followed by No 96 Squadron by the end of 1941 and later by Nos 125, 256 and 410 Squadrons. Production of the Defiant I had now ceased, with a total of 712 aircraft, and the Defiant II had replaced it on the production line. The Defiant NF Mk II was used by Nos 141, 151 and 153 Squadrons, the last aircraft being delivered in February 1942.

Intruders

One principal headache for the RAF's night defence in 1940–41 was German intruder operations over the United Kingdom. In mid-May 1940, in the wake of the German *Blitzkrieg* in France and the Low Countries, Royal Air Force Bomber Command had begun operations for the first time against oil and communications targets in Germany, having hitherto confined itself to fringe attacks directed mainly against naval facilities. Such raids, mounted in growing strength, were intolerable to the Nazi leadership and in particular to *Reichsmarschall* Hermann Goering, the *Luftwaffe* C-in-C, who had earlier boasted that if enemy bombs ever fell on the *Reich* territory people might call him Meier – a predominantly Jewish name.

It is untrue, as has sometimes been suggested, that the *Luftwaffe*'s pre-war planners had given no thought to the night defence of Germany. Even before the war, an Me 109 squadron at Greifswald was assigned to night fighting practice with the aid of searchlights, and a specialist night fighter unit, 10/JG 26, also equipped with Me 109s, was on the order of battle in September 1939, although it was very much experimental and was not used operationally.

The unsuitability of the Me 109 for night fighter operations quickly became apparent, and following the start of the RAF's strategic offensive the first effective night fighter units were formed, equipped in the main with Me 110s. In addition to these, a specialist long-range night fighter unit, 1/NJG2,

Beaufighter Mk IIF of No 225 Squadron. This unit served in the UK and the Middle East. (Philip Jarrett)

was also established with three squadrons of Ju 88s and one of Do 17s. Tasked with long-range night fighter operations, this was the *Luftwaffe*'s first night intruder *Gruppe*, and early in August 1940 it deployed forward to Gilze-Rijn in Holland, from where it began operations against the British Isles in September under the command of *Hauptmann* Karl-Heinrich Heyse.

The *Gruppe*'s operational area over Britain was divided into three sectors. Sector One covered an area bounded by the Thames estuary, north London, the east Midlands and the Wash, taking in the whole of East Anglia; Sector Two ran inland from the Wash to Birmingham, then swung north to Sheffield and north-east to the Humber, covering Lincolnshire and south Yorkshire; while Sector Three ran from the Humber to Sheffield, Sheffield to Leeds, Leeds to Blackpool and finally from Blackpool to a point on the Northumbrian coast north of Newcastle-upon-Tyne. This was the only sector to extend as far as the west coast and was the largest in area – although by no means the most important, as the other two encompassed the two areas where Bomber Command had its densest concentration of airfields.

After some preliminary sorties over Lincolnshire

Beaufighter Mk I seen in 1940 with the first 'thimble' nose radome developed for the AI Mk VII centimetric radar. (Philip Jarrett)

R227, one of two Beaufighter Mk IIs experimentally fitted with a four-gun turret just behind the cockpit. (Philip Jarrett)

in late August 1940, the intruders claimed their first confirmed victory on 21 September, when *Hauptmann* Karl Hulshoff destroyed a Whitley of No 58 Squadron, the aircraft crashing near Thornaby with the loss of all four crew. Three nights later, *Feldwebel* Hans Hahn shot down a No 102 Squadron Whitley near Linton-on-Ouse. In the early hours of 28 September Lindholme was attacked by *Leutnant* Heinz Volker, who damaged a Hampden of No 49 Squadron as it was landing and shot down a second just off the coast.

During this initial period of operations the intruders lost four aircraft, although only one is thought to have been destroyed by the air defences – in this instance by anti-aircraft fire. During October and November the sortie rate was low, but in December several sorties were flown against the Lincolnshire airfields, in the course of which a Do 17 was destroyed and another damaged by Hurricanes of No 12 Group flying night patrols. During one of these sorties, the *Gruppe* commander, *Major* Karl-Heinrich Heyse, was shot down and killed by the Manby airfield defences.

In December 1940 No 4 Operational Training Unit – later renamed No 54 OTU – was established at Church Fenton to train night fighter crews. It may be that *Luftwaffe* Intelligence got wind of the OTU's activities, because on the night of 15 January 1941 the station was attacked by an intruding Ju 88 of NJG2, which badly damaged two Defiants and a Blenheim. Earlier in the month, another intruder had also attacked and badly damaged a No 10 Squadron Whitley near Catterick.

On 10/11 February 1941 the intruders threw their weight against the Lincolnshire airfields of No 5 Group, destroying seven aircraft returning from raids on Germany and Holland. Despite

encounters with RAF night fighters, all the intruders – nine aircraft – returned to base.

Since November 1940, No 600 Squadron, which had brought its Blenheim night fighters north to Catterick in the previous month, had been in the process of conversion to Beaufighters; it was declared operational in March 1941, when it moved to Drem for a fortnight before departing for Colerne in Wiltshire. Another Beaufighter squadron, No 68, also formed at Catterick early in the year, but in April it was assigned to the defence of the Midlands.

Also in the north, one Defiant squadron, No 141, was based at Ayr from the end of April 1941, and – with detachments at Acklington – found itself in the middle of the May 'Blitz' on Clydeside and Tyneside, its crews claiming eight victories. Although still not radar-equipped, the Defiant was proving itself unexpectedly suited to the night fighter role; experience had taught crews that if the pilot could manoeuvre his aircraft to a position beneath an enemy bomber, the gunner, elevating his guns at an angle, could usually inflict punishing damage on it. As mentioned elsewhere, it was a technique developed further by the *Luftwaffe*'s night fighter force later in the war, when aircraft fitted with upwards-firing guns inflicted severe losses on the RAF's heavy bombers.

The inauguration of Ground Controlled Interception (GCI) stations such as that at Patrington, on the Humber estuary, and the conversion of five of Fighter Command's six Blenheim squadrons to Beaufighters in March 1941, brought about a dramatic change in the Command's fortunes just in time to counter the *Luftwaffe*'s 'Blitz' on London, Merseyside, Tyneside, Clydeside and other targets. The Hurricane and Defiant squadrons allocated to night defence also added to

Beaufighter Mk VI in night fighter finish and with a flat tailplane; later production Mk VIs had dihedral on the tailplane. The Mk VI was the first Beaufighter variant to equip RAF squadrons in India. (Philip Jarrett)

this change as a result of their increased experience, and because they too derived assistance from GCI. The much more precise information provided by the GCI stations made the task of interception far easier, and matters improved still further with the introduction of AI Mk VII, which had a seven-mile range and a low-level capability. For the first time, the Mk VII, together with information passed on by the Chain Home Low radar stations – the low-level part of the general warning system – gave night fighter crews the ability to intercept low-flying minelayers and reconnaissance aircraft which had been operating off the north and east coasts almost with impunity.

The figures themselves reveal the general improvement in the overall air defence system by the summer of 1941. In February the enemy lost only four aircraft to fighters and eight to anti-aircraft, but during March night fighters shot down twenty-two enemy bombers and the AA guns seventeen. In April the score rose to forty-eight for the fighters and thirty-nine for the guns, and in the first two weeks of May the loss rate assumed serious proportions, ninety-six bombers being shot down by fighters and thirty-two by AA guns. In addition, ten others were lost due to unknown causes.

Following a final spate of intense attacks on London, the Midlands and Merseyside, the *Luftwaffe*'s spring 'Blitz' on Britain gradually petered out at the end of May 1941 as the Germans transferred the bulk of their bomber force to the

east in readiness for Operation *Barbarossa*, the invasion of Russia, or to the Balkans. Although bombing attacks on the north continued on a sporadic basis during 1941, these tended to follow intruder-type tactics, only small numbers of aircraft being involved.

As for the dedicated intruder squadrons, these continued to concentrate on the bomber bases of Lincolnshire and East Anglia in the spring of 1941, and forays into northern airspace were few. Nevertheless, they did occur, and on the night 16/17 April a Ju 88 flown by *Feldwebel* Wilhelm Breetz, one of NJG2's most experienced pilots, fell victim to the Tyne anti-aircraft defences. Another experienced intruder pilot, *Leutnant* Heinz Volker, had better luck in the early hours of 26 April, destroying a Blenheim and a Defiant at Church Fenton and damaging two more aircraft in a combined bombing and strafing attack. Volker also claimed two more aircraft destroyed that night in attacks on the Lincolnshire airfields.

Intruder attacks continued during June and were again directed against Lincolnshire and East Anglia, but on the night 13/14th the intruders suffered a severe setback when three Ju 88s failed to return, all falling victim to the Beaufighters of No 25 Squadron from Wittering. This was not, however, by any means the beginning of the end for the intruders; Beaufighters accounted for only three more before the middle of October, although others fell to anti-aircraft fire and, in one case, to a

Although the Dornier 17 was the type used in early German intruder operations over the British Isles, it was later replaced by the Junkers Ju 88, pictured here. (Author)

Douglas Havoc night fighter of No 85 Squadron.

What spelled the end of intruder operations over England was a personal instruction from Adolf Hitler on 13 October 1941, ordering them to cease. The reason was purely one of propaganda. With the RAF's night-bombing effort steadily increasing, Hitler wanted the German people to see the 'terror bombers' destroyed over *Reich* territory; far-away victories over England did nothing to improve their morale. For *General* Kammhuber, commanding Germany's night defences, it was a bitter blow; what was potentially his most potent weapon had been struck from his hand, and no argument would sway the *Führer*.

What, then, had the intruder force – which never numbered more than twenty or thirty serviceable aircraft – achieved in just over a year of operations?

It had certainly destroyed more than fifty aircraft over England, together with an estimated thirty more over the North Sea. About forty others sustained damage as a consequence of intruder attacks. The cost to the Germans was twenty-seven aircraft, plus seven more destroyed in accidents.

Had the *Luftwaffe* been permitted to step up its intruder operations over the United Kingdom in the winter of 1941–42, as RAF Bomber Command prepared to launch a renewed offensive against Germany with its four-engined heavy bombers, it might have dealt a series of damaging blows to the Command, both materially and in terms of morale. It would return to intruder operations later in the war, but by then the intruders would have to contend with air defences vastly superior to those they had encountered previously.

CHAPTER FIVE

THE NIGHT DEFENCE OF GERMANY, 1940–42

At the beginning of World War II, although Germany had an air defence system in place, the emphasis was largely on anti-aircraft artillery, and a lot of misplaced faith was pinned on the ability of the *Fliegerabwehrkanone* (flak) units to defend the air space of the *Reich*. This was mainly a consequence of German experiences in the Spanish Civil War, where flak had proved very effective against low-flying aircraft; the fact that air power in Spain, apart from a few much-publicised attacks on cities, had been used almost exclusively in the tactical role, and that anti-aircraft weaponry would not be anything like as effective against high-flying targets, was ignored.

Fighters, according to the prevailing doctrine, were there for an altogether different purpose, which was to conduct offensive operations in enemy air space. The task of the bomber and fighter units of an air fleet (*Luftflotte*) was to co-operate closely with one another in support of ground campaigns. Each air fleet had to operate in concert with an army group; it was, in effect, a small self-contained air force operating within a defined area, and

its commander-in-chief was responsible for both offensive and defensive operations within that area. This meant that when an army group was on the offensive in enemy territory, the C-in-C of the air fleet supporting it still remained responsible for the air defence of his original assigned region in Germany.

The Germans were very slow to recognise the need for a centralised system of air defence, probably made complacent by the speed of their early conquests, but with British night bombers attacking targets on the territory of the *Reich* during and after the Battle of France there was a clear requirement for a night air defence system based on fighters as well as flak, and in July 1940 the *Luftwaffe* established the 1st Night Fighter Division in Brussels under *General* Josef Kammhuber.

On 26 June 1940, just after the end of the fighting in France, the commander of 1/*Zerstörergeschwader* 1 (1/ZG1) was summoned to a high-level conference in The Hague. His name was *Hauptmann* Wolfgang Falck, and he had recently completed a lengthy report on attempts by his unit, which was

The Messerschmitt 110 became the Luftwaffe's *standard night fighter type in 1940, but initially crews were handicapped by a lack of AI radar.* (Author)

armed with Me 110s, to intercept British bombers passing over its base at Aalborg, in Denmark. Falck had trained his best crews in instrument flying and had held a battle flight on readiness every night, hoping to catch the elusive bombers with the help of a *Freya* radar station off the north German coast (an experimental unit that had been operating on the island of Wangerooge since the autumn of 1939).

The crews had met with no success, but they were the only fighter aircrew in the *Luftwaffe* with substantial experience of night flying, and the upshot of the meeting was that Falck was appointed to command the first night fighter *Geschwader*, NJG1, to be formed out of a *Gruppe* of ZG1 and one of JG2 (4/JG2, which had just converted from Me 109s to Me 110s.) These were now re-designated 1/NJG1, under *Hauptmann* Radusch, and 3/NJG1, under Major Blumensaat. In addition, a second *Gruppe*, 1/NJG2, was also formed under *Hauptmann* Karl-Heinrich Heyse, primarily for intruder operations over Britain; its activities have already been discussed.

It was apparent that NJG1's night fighters, lacking any aid to interception other than the eyesight of their crews, would have to co-operate closely with searchlights and sound locators. A belt of these was already in place on an oblique line west of Munster; Kammhuber now ordered it to be extended to north and south until it stretched for some twenty-five miles along the approach to the Ruhr. Individual fighters were each allocated a sector within this belt, orbiting a radio beacon, their crews hoping to pick up a bomber once the searchlights were illuminated.

It was hardly surprising that the night fighters registered few successes with these tactics, and it was not until October 1940, with the introduction of the first *Wurzburg* fighter-direction radars, that matters began to improve. The system was somewhat cumbersome, involving a *Freya* station to provide early warning, and two *Wurzburgs*, one to track the incoming bomber and the other to direct the night fighter. The biggest snag with the whole system was that only one fighter could be controlled at any one time within each sector, and the fighter could not be handed over from one sector to another. The fighter controller could bring the interceptor to within a mile or so of its target, but it was in that last mile – with the fighter pilot depending on his eyesight alone – that the problems really began. Often, despite the fact that they knew they were within a few hundred yards of the bomber, the night fighters failed to intercept. When they did so, it was with a large element of luck. On the night 16/17 October 1940, for example, *Oberleutnant* Ludwig Becker, commanding 6/NJG2, and his radio operator, *Feldwebel* Staub, made the first successful ground-controlled interception of an enemy aircraft, assisted by

The German night fighters' principal opponent early in 1941 was the Vickers Wellington. The aircraft seen here belong to No 9 Squadron, whose motto was – and still is – Per Noctem Volamus *(We Fly By Night).* (Author)

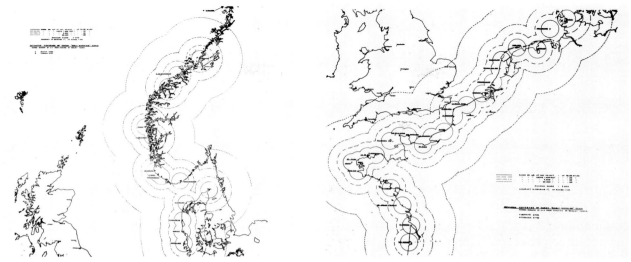

Diagram showing the German early warning radar coverage in 1942, according to a British intelligence assessment. It turned out to be quite accurate. (Author)

information from a *Freya* set passed to them by the fighter controller, *Oberleutnant* Werner Schulze. They destroyed their target, a Wellington, but it was by pure chance that they spotted the bomber's exhaust flames in the night sky.

The night fighters' chances of success decreased in the spring of 1941, for the weight of Bomber Command's offensive was concentrated on the French Channel ports over a period of several weeks. When the main offensive again switched to German industrial targets in May the night fighter crews once more had their chance to score, and on the night 2/3 June 1941 an Me 110 crew, *Feldwebels* Kalinowski and Zwickl, became the first to destroy an enemy bomber – a Short Stirling – over the German capital, Berlin.

On 27/28 June, when seventy-three Wellingtons and thirty-five Whitleys were despatched to attack Bremen, returning crews reported, for the first time, that they had been subjected to intense night fighter attacks. Encountering bad weather, many crews attacked Hamburg in error, and five Whitleys were shot down by night fighters over the city – four of them by *Oberleutnant* Eckardt of 2/NJG1, the biggest success so far by a German night fighter pilot. Night fighters accounted for a further three bombers over Hamburg two nights later.

By mid-July 1941 the German night fighter force had 134 twin-engined fighters deployed in the west, and trained crews were reaching the *Staffeln* in growing numbers. On 1 August the 1st Night-Fighter Division was given Air Corps (*Fliegerkorps*) status, and Kammhuber set up a new HQ at Zeist, near Utrecht. The air defence system underwent a substantial reorganisation with the creation of the so-called 'Kammhuber Line'. This comprised a searchlight and flak belt, about twenty-two miles deep, and an overlapping network of circular air

defence zones (known as *Himmelbett*, or 'four poster bed' zones) extending along the North Sea coast from Denmark to Belgium. From north-east to south-west the zones were code-named *Pelikan*, *Hummer* (Lobster), *Kuckuck* (Cuckoo), *Wal* (Whale), *Languste* (Spiny Lobster), *Jaguar*, *Delphin* (Dolphin), *Schlei* (Tench), *Löwe* (Lion), *Tiger*, *Eisbär* (Polar Bear), *Salzhering* (Salt Herring), *Hering*, *Zander* (Pike), *Seeadler* (Sea Eagle), *Rotkehlchen* (Redbreast), *Biber* (Beaver), *Gorilla*, *Schmetterling* (Butterfly), *Hamster*, *Bremse* (Horsefly) and *Wespe* (Wasp). A further searchlight and flak belt and nine more *Himmelbett* zones protected Berlin, while joint night fighter and flak zones were set up to defend the industrial areas of the Ruhr.

The system was as tightly controlled as Kammhuber could make it, but the fact remained that each ground controller could still only direct a single fighter, whose pilot then had to rely on his vision to make contact with the target; but this deficiency was about to be put right. As early as July 1939 the German communications firm, Telefunken, had shown that it was possible for an intercepting aircraft to be fitted with AI equipment, and had carried out a practical demonstration with a rudimentary set mounted in a Ju 52. The *Luftwaffe* Technical Office, however, had shown no interest in the device, and so Telefunken had developed it into a radar altimeter.

The AI concept was resurrected in the summer of 1940 and development went ahead, but there were a lot of snags to be overcome. One of them was that an internally-mounted antenna produced too weak a signal, so Telefunken had no choice but to opt for an externally-mounted aerial array – a far from satisfactory arrangement, not least because of the drag it produced.

In July 1941 a prototype set, named *Lichtenstein*, 53

Lichtenstein *AI radar installed in a Messerschmitt 110.* (Philip Jarrett)

was installed in a Me 110 based at Leeuwarden, Holland. On 9 August this aircraft, crewed by *Oberleutnant* Ludwig Becker and *Feldwebel* Josef Staub, intercepted a Wellington bomber with the aid of *Lichtenstein* and shot it down. Despite this success, Kammhuber had to maintain constant pressure to have his night fighters fitted with AI radar, and it was not until early in 1942 that *Lichtenstein*-equipped aircraft began to reach the night fighter wings (*Nachtjagdgeschwader*) in any numbers. Once they did, the effectiveness of the German night fighter force increased immeasurably, and some pilots began to achieve quite remarkable scores. One of them was *Hauptmann* Werner Streib, commanding 1/NJG1 at Venlo, who – accompanied by his observer, *Gefreiter* Lingen – had destroyed his first bomber, a Whitley, on the night 20/21 July 1940 while flying an Me 110. In August 1941 Streib destroyed three more bombers, and on the night 1/2 October he intercepted and destroyed three Wellingtons inside forty minutes.

Streib went on to gain sixty-six victories, and for a long time he was Germany's top-scoring night fighter pilot; but close behind him came *Leutnant* Helmut Lent, a veteran Me 110 pilot who had fought over Poland, Norway and in the defence of Germany against the early (and disastrous) daylight raids on the north German ports by RAF Bomber Command. On 1 November 1941, Lent formed a new night fighter *Gruppe*, 2/NJG2; his *Staffel* commanders were *Hauptmann* Rudolf Schönert, *Hauptmann* Prince Lippe-Weissenfeld, and *Hauptmann* Ludwig Becker. All of them went on to

achieve exceptional night fighting scores. Helmut Lent destroyed 102 aircraft at night and eight by day before his death in a flying accident on 7 October 1944; Lippe-Weissenfeld got fifty-one before his death in action on 12 March, 1944; and Becker had forty-six kills when he too was shot down, in February 1943. (See Appendix Two.)

Unfortunately for Germany's cities, Kammhuber's efforts to expand and streamline the night air defence system, and the growing prowess of his pilots, received scant attention in the corridors of the *Luftwaffe* High Command, preoccupied as it was with the German offensives in Russia. But there were some nasty shocks to come, beginning with a devastating incendiary attack by 191 RAF bombers on Lübeck on the night 28/29 March 1942 in which 200 acres of the Old Town were wiped out and sixty-two per cent of the town's buildings destroyed or damaged.

The raid represented Bomber Command's first major success against a German target, and it was followed in April by two major attacks on the Baltic port of Rostock and the adjacent Heinkel aircraft factory. Much damage was caused, and in reporting the raids the expression *Terrorangriff* (terror attack) was used for the first time by German radio announcers. The attacks still did not provoke major consternation, even though the German Propaganda Minister, Goebbels, noted in his diary that 'Community life in Rostock was practically at an end,' but there was much worse to come.

On the night 30/31 May, 1942, Bomber Command despatched 1,047 aircraft to Cologne. A

Dornier Do 217J-2 night fighter equipped with FuG202 Lichtenstein *B/C radar. The night fighter version of the Do 217 was used in small numbers in 1942–3.* (Philip Jarrett)

Cologne Cathedral stands forlornly amid the ruins of the ancient Rhineland city. (Author)

total of 868 aircraft bombed the main target area, dropping 1,455 tons of bombs, two-thirds of which were incendiaries. The city suffered very severe damage and the death toll was 469, the highest in any Bomber Command raid so far. Over 600 acres of Cologne's built-up area were destroyed, and about 250 factories were destroyed or badly damaged. The toll of property included 18,432 houses, apartments, workshops and public buildings destroyed and 40,586 damaged. Fifty per cent of the city's power supply was put out of action, and the gas and water supplies were seriously disrupted. The railway repair shops, employing 2,500 people, were totally destroyed and 12,000 fires were started, some of which burned for days. Bomber Command sustained a record loss of forty-one aircraft, of which twenty-nine were Wellingtons. Thirty-six were accounted for by fighters.

The massive onslaught demonstrated the limitations of the German air defence system, and Kammhuber strove to improve it still further. The coverage of the *Himmelbett* zones was extended; new night fighter *Gruppen* were formed, and new methods were introduced which permitted ground controllers to direct two fighters within a single zone. But the supply of night fighters was slow; the number deployed in September 1942 was 345, only ninety-five more than the figure for September 1941.

Despite mounting further raids involving 1,000 bombers in 1942, Bomber Command was unable to repeat the success of the Cologne attack. Had it done so, it is probable that Germany's leaders would have placed high priority on the massive reinforcement of the night fighter arm in 1942, with disastrous consequences for the RAF's night offensive in late 1942 and early 1943.

As it was, it would take a fearsome onslaught on Hamburg in July 1943 to bring about that result; and although subsequent events would bring the *Nachtjagdgeschwader* to a high point of effectiveness, it would not spare Germany's cities the ordeal that was yet to come.

CHAPTER SIX

NIGHT DEFENCE OF THE UK, JANUARY 1942-JUNE 1944

At the end of 1941 nine squadrons of Beaufighters were assigned to the night defence of Britain, one having formed during the summer and three having converted from Defiants. The squadrons were Nos 25 at Wittering (Northamptonshire), 29 at West Malling (Kent), 68 at High Ercall (Shropshire), 141 at Drem (East Lothian), 219 at Tangmere (Sussex), 255 at Coltishall (Norfolk), 307 at Exeter (Devon), 60 at Predannack (Cornwall) and 604 at Middle Wallop (Hampshire).

Six Defiant night fighter squadrons were also still on the Order of Battle. They were Nos 96 at Wrexham (Denbighshire), 125 at Fairwood Common (Glamorgan), 151 at Coltishall, 153 at Ballyhalbert (Co Down), 256 at Coltishall, and 264 at West Malling.

Added to these was No 85 Squadron at Hunsdon in Hertfordshire, equipped with Douglas Havocs. These aircraft were converted Douglas DB-7 bombers, part of a batch originally intended for France. The aircraft had been selected for the night fighter role because it had a good performance, a tricycle undercarriage – which made night landings and take-offs simpler – and its roomy interior readily lent itself to the fitting of AI radar.

Modification of the DB-7 (or Boston, as it was known in the RAF) was undertaken at Burtonwood, and two versions emerged. Both were known as the Havoc Mk I, but one featured a 'solid' nose containing eight .303 in machine-guns and was equipped with AI Mk IV radar; the other retained the transparent nose of the DB-7 and was in effect a night intruder, with four extra machine-guns in

The Douglas Havoc II in its basic night fighting form, with AI Mk IV radar and a twelve-gun nose. The gun ports are patched over in this photograph. Only No 85 Squadron operated this version. (Philip Jarrett)

Havoc Mk I of No 93 Squadron. This unit carried out experiments with various night fighting techniques, including the dropping of mines on enemy bombers. No 93 Squadron was the first to receive the Havoc. (Philip Jarrett)

the nose and no AI for obvious security reasons. This version was issued to No 23 Squadron at Ford, Hampshire, in March 1941; a few were also used by No 25 Squadron at Wittering between July and September 1941.

The first squadron to use the Havoc was No 93, which in December 1941 was in the process of disbanding at RAF Middle Wallop. No 93 Squadron had spent most of its career engaged in a series of rather bizarre experiments involving the dropping of aerial mines on enemy bombers; these had first been carried out in 1940, using Handley Page

A Havoc II (Turbinlite) of No 1459 Flight, showing the AI Mk IV radar aerials around the nose installation of the searchlight itself. Much time was wasted in experimenting with this quite useless arrangement. (Philip Jarrett)

Cockpit of the Mosquito NF Mk II, showing the observer's AI radar tube on the right-hand side. Positioning the radar operator alongside the pilot and not, as in the Blenheim and Beaufighter, at a remote location in the fuselage significantly improved crew teamwork. (Philip Jarrett)

Harrows. Havocs so modified were designated Havoc Mk I (LAM), the abbreviation standing for Long Aerial Mine. These operations, known as *Mutton*, were a predictable waste of time and effort, as was the Havoc I (Turbinlite). Trials with this had begun in May 1941 with the specially-formed No 1422 Flight. They involved the installation of a 2,700 million candlepower Helmore/GEC search-light in the Havoc's nose, together with the AI Mk V. No armament was carried, the idea being that the Havoc would detect an enemy bomber, close in on it, and then illuminate it with the searchlight so that an accompanying Hurricane or Defiant could shoot it down. Ten Turbinlite flights were formed in 1941 following protracted development caused by many technical and operational difficulties, and remained operational throughout 1942, being given squadron identities (Nos 530–539) before they were eventually disbanded in January 1943. Between them they only succeeded in destroying one aircraft, and that was a Stirling of No 218 Squadron. Luckily, its crew escaped.

The real answer to the prayers of the RAF night fighter squadrons was the de Havilland Mosquito. The first Mosquito fighter squadron, No 157,

formed at Debden in Essex on 13 December 1941, its first aircraft, a dual-control Mk II, arriving at Debden's satellite airfield, Castle Camps, on 26 January 1942. Seventeen Mk IIs were delivered to Maintenance Units for the fitting of AI Mk V, and by mid-April No 157 Squadron had nineteen NF Mk IIs on its inventory, three of them without radar. By this time No 151 Squadron at Wittering had also begun to rearm with the NF Mk II, with sixteen aircraft on strength at the end of April.

As the two squadrons built up their night flying hours, practised interceptions and night gun-firing (which revealed the need for flash eliminators on the nose-mounted .303 in Browning guns, which, when fired, blinded the pilot to everything outside the cockpit) the crews became increasingly happy with their new aircraft. Its armament of four 20 mm Hispano cannon and four Brownings was formidable, and – unlike the arrangement in the Beaufighter – the radar observer sat facing forwards in the cockpit, on the pilot's right and slightly behind him.

Crews were less than happy, however, with the AI Mk V. As one No 157 Squadron radar operator, Squadron Leader Lewis Brandon, DSO, DFC, put

These early production Mosquito NF Mk IIs were delivered to the RAF in February-March 1944. (Philip Jarrett)

it in *Night Flyer*, published by William Kimber in 1961:

'Fighter Command had committed a blunder almost as bad as the Turbinlite fiasco. They had decided to install in our beautiful Mozzies, in fact in all the first batch of Mozzies to reach squadrons, a wretched new mark of AI. This was the Mark 5 AI, which had all the faults of the early Mark 4 plus many of its own. It was a retrograde step even when compared with Mark 4, but when compared with Mark 7 it was like going back to a divining-rod. There were times in the next few months when I thought that if I took a hazel twig, persuaded a Dachshund to lift a leg against it and then took the twig into the Mozzie with me, it would lead me to a German more readily than would Mark 5 AI.

'It had been wished on to Fighter Command by the experts of the Fighter Interception Unit. While it might have been all very well for these highly skilled pilots, it was not very practical for the average squadron pilot. It had the same aerial system as Mark 4 and the main difference was that it had an extra tube, placed so that the pilot could see it and could carry out the final stages of the interception himself. All the navigator needed to do was to read out the range. At night the pilot had his hands full enough without giving him an extra tube to look at. Then, too, when he should have been searching the sky for a visual, he would have to look at this indicator tube. Apart from these points, the equipment suffered from very serious limitations that were not discovered until we had been struggling with it for several months ... Unfortunately a large number of sets had been made and it took some time to get them replaced.'

It was unfortunate that the Mosquito crews had to cope with inadequate equipment, for on the night 23/24 April the *Luftwaffe* launched the first of its so-called 'Baedecker' raids against British targets of cultural and historic value in reprisal for the Bomber Command attack on Lübeck on 28/29 March. The first raid, on Exeter by forty-five aircraft – mostly Do 217s of KG2 – proved abortive and was followed by two on Bath on 25 and 26 April. The city suffered heavily, and in three more successive raids Norwich was attacked twice and York once, the latter city suffering heavy damage from incendiary bombs. The most successful attack was on 3/4 May, when 131 tons of bombs were dropped on Exeter, severely damaging the city centre. During the remainder of the month Cowes, Norwich, Hull, Poole, Canterbury and Grimsby were all raided, but then the emphasis switched to more important strategic targets such as Birmingham, Southampton and Middlesbrough.

Although the two Mosquito night fighter squadrons made several contacts with enemy

(Trans) The speedy Dornier 217 was the Mosquito night-fighters' main target during the 'Baedecker' raids of early 1942. (Author)

aircraft during the first month of the German offensive, the Beaufighter squadrons remained in the forefront of the action, and it was not until 29 May that the first successful interception was made by a Mosquito, during a raid on Grimsby. At 04.30 Flight Lieutenant Pennington of No 151 Squadron was vectored on to an He 111 and opened fire on it over the North Sea. The Heinkel, with one engine on fire, spiralled down into the haze and

Pennington lost it, claiming it as a probable. His own aircraft was damaged by return fire and he flew back to base on one engine. In another incident, Pilot Officer Wain damaged a Do 217E, and on 30 May Squadron Leader Ashfield of No 157 Squadron damaged a Do 217 off Dover.

On 3 May No 264 Squadron began to rearm with Mosquitoes at Colerne, Wiltshire, the squadron flying its first night combat patrol on the 13th.

A standard Mosquito Mk II night fighter, DD750. This aircraft was delivered to the RAF in September 1942 and subsequently served with Nos 151, 264, 157, 410 and 239 Squadrons before being damaged beyond repair on operations on 28 June 1944. (Philip Jarrett)

It was not until the end of June that the Mosquito night fighters scored their first confirmed victories. On the night 24/25 June, aircraft of No 151 Squadron accounted for two Do 217E4s, shooting down a Dornier of 2/KG40 into the North Sea and another into the Wash. The squadron claimed two more enemy aircraft, an He 111 and a Do 217, before the end of the month, but there is no confirmation of these claims in records of enemy losses.

It was a frustrating time for No 157 Squadron; despite numerous patrols, its crews failed to score a confirmed victory until 22/23 August, when Wing Commander Gordon Slade and Pilot Officer Truscott shot down a Do 217 of 2/KG2 at Worlington, Suffolk. The Beaufighter crews were still claiming the lion's share of success, but that would soon change as more Mosquito squadrons formed. Number 85 Squadron began rearming with Mosquitoes in August, followed by Nos 25 and 410 Squadrons in October. Number 25 Squadron became the first Mosquito night fighter squadron in northern England, moving to Church Fenton and displacing No 54 OTU, which went to Charterhall on the Scottish Borders. Number 410 Squadron, at Acklington in Northumberland,

became responsible for the night defence of Tyneside.

The advent of the Mosquito was timely, for KG2's fast Dorniers, which were capable of 300 mph at low altitude, were causing problems for the defences. And it was not only historic towns that were hit; Middlesbrough, for example, after a break of five months, was attacked four times between the middle of April and the end of July 1942. It is also worth recording that, outside the great conurbations of London and Merseyside, the hardest-hit city in Britain was Hull. By the war's end, only 6,000 out of 93,000 buildings in Hull had escaped bomb damage, most of it incurred during three major attacks in March and May 1941. Because of its geographical location, Hull was an easy target. It was heavily attacked twice during Operation *Steinbock*, the so-called 'Little Blitz' of January to May 1944, conducted by all available German bombers on the Western Front. During these two attacks, carried out by Ju 88s, Do 217s and He 177s, No 25 Squadron (Coltishall), 264 Squadron (Church Fenton) and 307 Polish Squadron (Drem) claimed eleven enemy aircraft between them. As a matter of note, the 'Little Blitz' cost the *Luftwaffe* 329

Mosquito victim: a Junkers Ju 88A-4 of 8/KG6 brought down by Flt Lt R.C. Pargeter and Flt Lt R.L. Fell of No 29 Squadron at Withyham, Sussex, on the night of 24/25 February 1944. Two crew members baled out and were taken prisoner. (Philip Jarrett)

aircraft, of which 129 were destroyed by Mosquitoes equipped with AI Mk VIII radar.

In 1943–4 the *Luftwaffe* once again mounted frequent intruder operations, using mainly Me 410 and Ju 188 aircraft. We can see a measure of what they might have achieved, had these aircraft been committed in greater numbers, in one attack on American air bases in East Norfolk on 2 April 1944, when intruders destroyed thirteen B-24 Liberators and, in the panic, two more were shot down by their own airfield defences. The Germans lost a single Me 410.

By the beginning of 1944, further improvements in the British air defences had made it hard for the *Luftwaffe* to penetrate UK air space at medium and low level. Increased numbers of anti-aircraft guns of all calibres, rocket batteries capable of firing salvoes of 128 missiles, and radar-directed searchlights able to illuminate targets up to 35,000 feet all contributed to frustrating the attackers, and the fast enemy bombers now began to penetrate at up to 30,000 feet before diving on their objectives and making a high-speed exit. These new tactics caused

problems for the night fighters, since following an enemy aircraft in a dive meant that radar contact was often lost because of ground returns. The answer was to extend the night fighter patrol lines well out to sea; many intruders were trapped and destroyed in this way.

Had the *Luftwaffe* been in a position to launch a renewed night offensive against the north in the early summer of 1944, it would not have been left entirely to the RAF to counter the threat. By this time, radar-equipped Fairey Fireflies of No 784 Squadron, Fleet Air Arm, were operating from Drem as part of the integrated air defence system. It is interesting to note that the Navy's Fireflies did in fact operate against night intruders – but that was in Korea, in 1951, when several aircraft were deployed to Kimpo to form a defence flight against Po-2 biplanes making night attacks on United Nations forces. No claims were made.

At Scorton, in North Yorkshire, the 422nd and 425th Squadrons of the US IXth Army Air Force, which had been training there for some weeks, were declared combat-ready early in June 1944.

Northrop P-61 Black Widows of the US IXth AAF were based at Scorton, Yorkshire, in 1944 before departing for the Continent.
(Philip Jarrett)

Serrate *installation in a Mosquito.* (Author)

Equipped originally with Beaufighters, these squadrons now had a full complement of Northrop P-61 Black Widow night fighters, and were also integrated with the air defence system before departing for the Continent in July.

Mention must be made of deception techniques, which contributed in no small measure to thwarting the enemy night offensive. By the end of 1941, airfields in the north and elsewhere were backed up by decoys known as 'Q' sites, with dummy flarepath and perimeter lighting laid out to resemble the pattern of the real aerodrome. According to some estimates, these decoy sites received seven times the number of bombs as those that fell on the real airfields. Most were closed down in the summer of 1944, when the bombing threat had receded.

Radio deception equipment was also installed; this included masking beacons, devised by the Radio Branch of the Post Office Engineering Department and designed to interfere with the *Luftwaffe*'s radio navigational aids. Three such beacons, known as Meacons, were situated in the North, at Marske near Redcar, Reston near Eyemouth and Mintlaw near Peterhead. They

achieved considerable success. On the night 6/7 July 1941, for example, thanks to the jamming of the Noordwijk beacon, three Ju 88s of *Kustenfliegergruppe* 106 operating between Holy Island and Whitby, became disorientated and all three flew into high ground near Bridlington.

By the beginning of 1943 the RAF's night fighter squadrons were turning increasingly from defence to offence. The Mosquito's long range and heavy armament of four 20 mm cannon made it highly suitable for the night-intruder role, as well as for local night air defence. The intruder Mosquitoes (and Beaufighters), although stripped of their AI for operations over enemy territory, were fitted with a device named *Serrate* which, developed by the Telecommunications Research Establishment as a result of information on enemy night fighting radars brought back by special countermeasures aircraft, enabled the British fighters to home in to the enemy's airborne radar transmissions. It had a range of about fifty miles, and was first used operationally in June 1943 by No 141 Squadron, which scored twenty-three kills in three months with its help.

Number 141 Squadron's commander was Wing Commander J.R.D. 'Bob' Braham, whose combat report describes a night action off the Dutch island of Ameland on 17/18 August 1943. Braham was flying a Beaufighter Mk VI, and his navigator was Flight Lieutenant H. Jacobs.

'We took off from Coltishall at 2200 hours on intruder patrol to Stade. We flew to a point north of Schiermonnikoog and then turned NE at 2254. We continued on course for about five minutes when we sighted one Me 110 flying east and jinking. We turned and followed him towards the coast, closing in on the aircraft until we were at 300 yards range, 20 degrees starboard astern and a little below. Fire was opened with a two-second burst from all guns and strikes were seen all over the enemy aircraft. Smoke came from the port engine and the Me 110 dived to port. We gave him another two-second burst from 250 yards and he caught fire and dived into the sea, burning on the water. Immediately afterwards we saw a second Me 110 (which had been chasing us) a little above and turning gently to starboard on an easterly course. We gave a one-second burst of cannon and machine gun at 50 yards in a gentle turn. The enemy aircraft appeared to blow up and we had to pull up and turn to port to avoid ramming it. At that point we saw one man bale out and his parachute open, and the enemy aircraft dived vertically into the sea in flames ... we landed at Wittering at 0145.'

Bob Braham, a pre-war regular RAF officer, had been involved in the development of night fighting techniques since the beginning of the war, and he destroyed his first victim – a Do 17 – while flying a Blenheim of No 29 Squadron on 24 August 1940. By July 1941 he had four kills to his credit, all at night, and he increased this score to six by the end of the year. During this period, his observer was Sergeant Gregory, who was later commissioned. After a rest from operations (during which, incidentally, they destroyed a Do 217 in a Beaufighter 'borrowed' while on a visit to their old squadron) they rejoined No 29 Squadron in July 1942, and in just a few weeks they destroyed three enemy bombers and damaged three more.

In October 1942 the Braham-Gregory team shot down a Ju 88 and a Do 217. In the following month, Braham was promoted and given command of No 141 Squadron, beginning night-intruder operations in June 1943. On his first such mission, on 14

A Mosquito Mk VI about to depart on an intruder sortie over Occupied Europe, 1944. (Author)

June, he shot down a Me 110, and by the end of September he had brought his score to twenty enemy aircraft destroyed, nineteen of them at night. He was now level with John Cunningham, but his second operational tour was at an end and it was not until February 1944 that he was again permitted to fly operationally, and then only on a limited basis, as Wing Commander (Night Operations) at HQ No 2 Group.

In the meantime, No 141 Squadron, together with Nos 169 and 239, had been transferred from Fighter Command to No 100 (Countermeasures) Group, the task of the three squadrons being bomber support. The Mosquito crews of Nos 169 and 239 Squadrons had no experience of *Serrate* operations; moreover, the Mosquito Mk II aircraft with which they were initially armed were worn out, and their operations had to be severely curtailed so that they could be re-engined with new Rolls-Royce Merlin 22s on a rotational basis. During their first three months of operations the three squadrons combined claimed only thirty-one enemy aircraft destroyed or damaged, and six of these were shot down by Bob Braham. In March 1944 No 100 Group's fighter force was joined by No 515 Squadron, operating Beaufighters and later Mosquito VIs. This unit, however, was not equipped with *Serrate*.

During this period, changing his tactics, Braham made six low-level daylight intruder sorties into occupied Europe in March and April 1944, and on five of these trips he destroyed seven enemy aircraft. On the first sortie on 5 March (he was now flying a Mosquito, borrowed from No 305 Squadron at Lasham) he shot down an He 177, the biggest aircraft he had so far destroyed. His run of luck came to an end on 25 June 1944, when, flying a No 21 Squadron Mosquito, he was hit by flak and had to make a forced landing on a sandbar near Ringkøbing, Denmark. He spent the rest of the war in prison camp, as did his Australian navigator, Flight Lieutenant Don Walsh. Braham's score at the time of his capture was twenty-nine confirmed kills, making him the leading RAF night fighter pilot. He was also the first RAF pilot ever to be awarded three DSOs and three DFCs.

During the early weeks of 1944 the AOC-in-C Bomber Command, Air Chief Marshal Sir Arthur Harris, had been making determined efforts to persuade the Air Staff to release more night fighter squadrons to No 100 Group as a matter of priority. In April he wrote a strong letter to the Vice Chief of the Air Staff in which he recommended the transfer of at least ten fighter squadrons to the Group; in the event, a conference convened at the Air Ministry on the 20th of that month decided to authorise the transfer of only two, Nos 85 and 157, both armed with Mosquitoes.

This meagre increase did little to improve the effectiveness of No 100 Group's night fighter force. One of the problems was that Mosquitoes equipped with the latest AI Mk VII/VIII radar were forbidden to operate over enemy territory, and the earlier Mk IV that equipped most of the 100 Group night fighters was subjected to increasing interference from enemy countermeasures. To make matters worse, the usefulness of *Serrate* was over. The German *Lichtenstein* AI radar on which it was designed to home had been replaced by the more advanced SN-2, which worked outside *Serrate's* frequency cover. The end result was frustration for the night fighter crews. In June 1944, for example, only one enemy aircraft was destroyed in the course of 140 sorties. The situation improved somewhat towards the end of 1944, when Mosquitoes equipped with the latest AI radar were cleared to operate over enemy territory, and the old *Serrate* Mk I was replaced by a new version, the Mk IV. Some aircraft were also equipped with a new device known as *Perfectos*, which emitted a pulse that triggered the IFF (Identification Friend/Foe) sets of German night fighters and enabled the Mosquitoes to home on to the answering signal.

Nevertheless, No 100 Group's fighter force never really succeeded in getting to grips with the enemy night fighters. Quite apart from equipment problems, the Mosquito crews were faced with the formidable task of operating deep inside enemy territory as complete free-lancers, with no help from other quarters. Furthermore, enemy fighters had to be intercepted before they entered the bomber stream, because once they were inside it, it was extremely difficult to make radar contact with them owing to the profusion of other echoes. The tactics employed by the Mosquitoes usually began with a bombing and cannon attack on enemy night fighter airfields a few minutes before the bomber stream entered the area of German GCI radar coverage. Other Mosquitoes would work on the flanks of the stream, about forty miles from it and at a higher altitude, in the hope of intercepting enemy fighters before they reached the bombers. As the bombers were on their way home, more Mosquito fighter bombers loitered in the vicinity of the German airfields, waiting to catch the night fighters as they came in to land.

Few of the RAF's night fighter crews received publicity; in fact, many night fighter pilots achieved notable successes and remained almost entirely unknown outside the Service, at least until after the war. One of them was Flight Lieutenant George Esmond Jamieson, a young New Zealand pilot who, on the night 29/30 July 1944, set up an Allied record by destroying four enemy aircraft in one night. He was flying a Mosquito of No 488 RNZAF Squadron on patrol over Normandy, and

The pressurised Mosquito NF Mk XV carried nose radar and a ventral gun pack. It was designed for high-altitude operations, was powered by two-stage Merlin 61 engines, and was used only by No 85 Squadron. (Philip Jarrett)

Above and following spread: *The last night fighter Mosquito used in WWII was the NF30, which entered service with No 219 Squadron in June 1944.* (Philip Jarrett)

his navigator was Flying Officer Norman Crookes. Jamieson's combat report tells part of the story.

'I was patrolling the Coutance-St Lo area when I saw an unidentified aircraft approaching head-on at 5,000 feet height. Against the dawn I saw that it was a Junkers 88 and as I turned hard to port I followed him as he skimmed through the cloud tops. I closed to 300 yards and there was a series of explosions from the ground caused by the Junkers dropping his bombs as he tried to get away. I gave two short bursts as we came to the next clear patch, and after a fire in the port engine and fuselage the Ju 88 went down through the clouds vertically, hitting the ground near Caen.'

As Jamieson looked down at the debris of the Ju 88, Norman Crookes detected another aircraft on his radar and steered the pilot towards it. As he 69 closed in, the unexpected happened: yet another Junkers suddenly burst out of the cloud, dead ahead of the Mosquito. The German pilot saw the danger and went into a diving turn, trying to regain the shelter of the clouds, but he was too late. Jamieson opened fire from a range of 350 yards, and flames were soon streaming back from the Junkers' starboard engine. The aircraft fell through the cloud layer, burning fiercely, and plunged into the ground.

'Almost immediately I obtained a brief visual on an aircraft crossing from port to starboard some 5,000 feet away and identified as a Ju 88. My navigator confirmed this and took over on his "box of tricks", keeping me behind the enemy aircraft, which was now taking violent evasive action and at the same time jamming our equipment. When we were down to almost treetop height I regained the visual at only 250 yards, opening fire immediately and causing the Junkers to pull up almost vertically, turning to port with sparks and debris falling away. The Ju eventually stalled and dived into a four-acre field where it exploded. This was near Lisieux and as the time was now 0515 hours I climbed back to 5,000 feet and requested control to vector me back to any activity, as I had already observed further anti-aircraft fire through the clouds ahead.'

The anti-aircraft fire, Jamieson soon established, was directed at a Do 217, whose pilot spotted the Mosquito as it closed in and began a series of violent evasive manoeuvres. Just as the Dornier was about to plunge into cloud, Jamieson opened fire and saw his shells bursting on the enemy's fuselage. The Dornier went down in flames, the rear gunner continuing to fire back almost until the bomber hit the ground.

Jamieson returned to New Zealand shortly after his exploit. His score was eleven enemy aircraft destroyed, one probably destroyed and two damaged, all of them at night or in weather conditions so bad that day fighters were unable to operate. Eight of the enemy bombers were shot down while trying to attack Allied forces in Normandy, and the four kills of 29 July were all achieved within twenty minutes.

One Mosquito night fighter/intruder team that enjoyed considerable success was Flight Lieutenant James Benson and Squadron Leader Lewis Brandon (navigator) of No 157 Squadron. Together, they scored seven confirmed kills, with a number of claims for aircraft probably destroyed and damaged, and also destroyed six V-1 flying bombs in the summer of 1944. On the night 11/12 September 1944, while flying bomber support operations with No 100 Group, they were flying over the island of Seeland, off the south-east coast of Denmark, when Brandon picked up a transmission from an enemy night fighter radar. A few moments later, he made contact with the suspect aircraft and steered Benson towards it. In the clear moonlight, the enemy was identified as a Ju 188; it was flying in broad circles, apparently orbiting a German radio beacon.

Benson slid in astern of the Ju 188 and fired a burst into it, seeing his 20 mm shells strike home on the night fighter's starboard wing root. The Ju 188 lost speed rapidly, its starboard engine catching fire, and Benson had to pull up sharply to avoid a collision. The Ju 188 was last seen plunging earthwards, streaming flames. At that moment, Brandon picked up another contact. It was a second Ju 188, and it had probably been engaged in a night fighting exercise with the first. Benson closed in rapidly and gave the Junkers a two-second burst; bright flames streamed back from the enemy's ruptured fuel tanks and it dropped away towards the Danish coast, shedding great chunks of wreckage. The Mosquito sped through the cloud of smoke and debris that the Junkers left in its wake; when Benson and Brandon returned to base they found their aircraft smothered in oil and scarred by pieces of flying metal.

Meanwhile, as the RAF's night intruders were fighting an increasingly successful battle in enemy skies, the home-based night fighter squadrons were fighting a defensive battle against the first of Hitler's 'revenge weapons' – the V-1 flying bomb.

CHAPTER SEVEN

'CONSIDER YOURSELVES EXPENDABLE'

The first V-1 flying bombs fell on British soil on 12 June 1944, and eleven squadrons of the Air Defence of Great Britain (as RAF Fighter Command was now known, albeit for a mercifully short period) were assigned to deal with the threat. Number 11 Group instituted so-called *Diver* patrols, which involved fighters patrolling along three clearly-defined lines: the first between Beachy Head and Dover, the second over the coast between Newhaven and Dover, and the third between Haywards Heath and Ashford. At the same time, nearly 400 anti-aircraft guns and 480 barrage balloons were deployed on the V-1s' approach route to London.

For the fighter pilots engaged in air defence against the V-1, the main problem was one of accurate response and accurate control. Their small margin of speed over the flying bombs, coupled with the short time available to make an interception, demanded that they should be quickly and accurately directed on to the V-1's course before the missile reached the gun and balloon belts. There was consequently a major problem of warning and control to be solved, because the network of radar stations, Observer Corps posts, telecommunications and Fighter Command operations rooms, which had evolved so successfully earlier in the war to counter attacks by piloted aircraft, became suddenly outmoded in the face of this new threat. The same was true of the defence system as a whole; it was not just a matter of improving the efficiency of the guns, searchlights, balloons and fighters as separate weapons, but of co-ordinating their activities. This co-ordination was vital, in particular, between guns and fighters.

As the Operations Room at No 11 Group HQ was fully occupied in controlling fighter activities over the Normandy beachhead in June 1944, all *Diver* defences were controlled by the Operations Room of the Biggin Hill sector. This was linked with the operations rooms of Anti-Aircraft Command in the *Diver* area, and all information from the radar stations and the Observer Corps was fed into it. However, the control that was exercised by Biggin Hill was general rather than specific; and much different from the procedure that had normally been employed in the defence against piloted aircraft where the direction of intercepting fighters was the responsibility of the Sector Operations Room. Instead, executive control of the patrolling fighters was vested in the same agencies that detected and plotted the flying bombs; the radar stations and the Observer Corps centres at Horsham and Maidstone were used as fighter direction stations. Similarly, Anti-Aircraft Command found it impracticable to control the firing of individual batteries from gun operations rooms, and so batteries were allowed to fire independently, except when the gun operations rooms ordered fire to cease – in order to safeguard friendly aircraft, for example.

The system worked in that it reduced the time between detection and interception, but it had to be supplemented by a set of standing orders designed to avoid mutual interference between guns, fighters and balloons. Weather, too, was a prime consideration. As early as 16 June Air Marshal Sir Roderic Hill, commanding the Air Defence of Great Britain (himself an accomplished pilot who flew sixty-two anti-*Diver* patrols, flying each type of defensive fighter in turn), decided that fighters would patrol over the Channel and the strip of land between the coast and the southern limit of the gun belt. They were permitted to pass over the gun belt only when in pursuit of a flying bomb, in which case the guns were not to open fire.

On 19 June it was decided that on days of very good visibility only the fighters would operate, and on bad days only the guns. On moderate days both guns and fighters would operate, each in their own areas. These principles were expanded on 26 June under the curious code-names of *Flabby*, *Spouse* and *Fickle*. In the case of *Flabby*, there was to be a total prohibition of gunfire when the weather was suitable for fighters; *Spouse*, which came into force when the weather was unsuitable for fighters, allowed complete freedom to the guns; and *Fickle*, in average weather conditions, permitted the guns to fire in the *Diver* belt up to 8,000 feet. Fighters were prohibited from entering the belt except when making a visual interception; outside the *Diver* belt fighters were given complete freedom of action, and light anti-aircraft guns were allowed to fire by day against visual targets if no fighters were present.

However, although these rules went some way towards tackling the problem, they did not solve it. Fighter pilots frequently reported that they had been engaged by the guns, and the gunners no less frequently reported that their shooting had been hindered by the presence of fighters.

By the end of June two new methods of controlling the ADGB fighters had been evolved, one for controlling the fighters over the Channel and the other for the direction of fighters patrolling over land. The first of these – the close control method – involved the direction of individual fighters by controllers located at radar stations on the coast. Approaching flying bombs were plotted in the control room of the radar station from which the controller, who was in R/T communication with the patrolling fighter, would issue detailed instructions on the bomb's course so as to bring the pilot into a position to intercept. The factor limiting the extent to which this method could be used was the number of control points available; by the middle of July only four radar stations – two at Fairlight near Hastings, one at Swingate and one at Beachy Head – were engaged in close control.

The main practical difficulty was that existing types of radar station could not, for technical reasons, provide sufficient early warning of an approaching bomb. The best of the stations rarely detected the bombs at ranges of more than fifty miles, which meant that the fighter had, even in theory, no more than six minutes in which to intercept before the bomb reached the coast.

In practice it was less; first because there was a substantial time lag between the initial detection of a bomb and the transmission of interception data from the fighter controller to the pilot, and secondly because patrols could not be carried out at the limit of the radar detection range because of the risk of being surprised by enemy fighters. In the Straits of Dover the ADGB fighters had three minutes at the outside in which to intercept a V-1 before the missile reached the Kent coast.

Despite the shortcomings, ADGB persevered with the close control method, because successful interceptions resulted in the bombs falling harmlessly into the sea. Over land, where there were no low-looking radar facilities, the running commentary method was used. The controllers using this technique were located at three radar stations – Beachy Head, Hythe and Sandwich – and two Observer Corps centres, Horsham and Maidstone. In the running commentary method, the position and course of the flying bombs was passed on the same R/T frequency to all patrolling fighters,

Hawker Tempest Mk V of No 501 Squadron, which fought at night against the V-1 flying bombs. (James Grottick)

Personnel of No 501 Squadron, autumn 1944, together with some attached Mosquito aircrew. Left to right, perched on aircraft: Flt Lt Panton; two unknowns, both RCAF: Flt Lt Monty Burton; Flt Lt Bob Stockburn; Flg Off Bill Polley and Flg Off Bennett. Two unknown Canadians are on the tailplane. Standing, left to right: W/O Woyjinsky (Polish); an Army liaison officer; Flt Lt Robb; Flt Lt Hansen; Squadron Ldr Parker-Rees; Flt Lt 'Ollie' Willis; three unknowns; Flt Lt Jimmy Grottick; and the IO, name unknown. (James Grottick)

whose pilots then worked out their own course to intercept the target. This method was also used for fighters patrolling seaward, but it worked best over land where shellbursts, rockets from ROC (Royal Observer Corps) posts, searchlight beams and landmarks all helped the pilots to make speedy interceptions. The chief drawback was that more than one fighter often went after the same flying bomb, a waste of effort which meant that some V-1s slipped through unmolested.

The Mosquito night fighter squadrons opened their score against the V-1s on the night 15/16 June 1944, when a Mosquito Mk VI of No 605 Squadron from Manston (Flight Lieutenant J.G. Musgrave and Flight Sergeant Sanewell) exploded one over the Channel. Musgrave reported that:

'... it was like chasing a ball of fire across the sky. It flashed by our starboard side a few thousand feet away at the same height as we were flying. I quickly turned to port and gave chase. It was going pretty fast, but I caught up with it and opened fire from astern. At first, there was no effect so I closed in another hundred yards and gave it another burst. Then I went closer still and pressed the button again. This

time, there was a terrific flash and explosion and the whole thing fell down in a vertical dive into the sea. The whole show was over in about three minutes.'

Four Mosquito squadrons – Nos 96, 219, 409 and 418 – were assigned exclusively to anti-*Diver* night patrols, and were joined later in June by Nos 85, 157 and 456, the first two temporarily reassigned from their intruder work. Other squadrons operated against the V-1s on a part-time basis, as priority was given to patrolling the Normandy beachhead. Between them, the seven full-time anti-*Diver* Mosquito squadrons claimed 471 flying bombs, while the part-timers claimed 152 to give a combined total of 623, or about one-third of the RAF's total claim against the V-1s.

Detachments of the USAAF's 422nd and 425th Squadrons also operated against the V-1s, their Black Widows being temporarily based at Hurn, but the crews were as yet inexperienced and they had little success, destroying nine flying bombs between them.

Although the ADGB's Mosquito squadrons bore the brunt of night operations against the V-1s, one

73

other squadron played an extraordinary part in the defence against the flying bombs. This was No 501 (County of Gloucester) Squadron, armed with Tempest Mk Vs. The story is told by one of the squadron's pilots, Flight Lieutenant A.J. 'Jimmy' Grottick, who took part in these activities from first to last.

'On 2 August 1944 No 501 Squadron moved to Manston. The unit was now fully equipped with Tempests, and the move was preparatory to crossing over to the Continent to join the Second Tactical Air Force. It was at this point that the axe fell. Several of us were seen – mainly those who had more night-flying hours in their log books than the others – and given an option.

'Either we could be reappointed to another operational unit, or we could go off for a rest period, probably as instructors on an operational training unit. Together with others given the option, I elected to remain operational.

'We were transferred from 501 Squadron on to what was known as a Fighter Interception Unit, also at Manston. So great had the V-1 menace become that it was decided to set up a special night fighter unit under the command of Squadron Leader Joe Berry. This, flying Tempests, would attempt to provide an effective response to V-1s coming in at night. At first, the FIU was just twelve pilots strong, but within about a week the loss rate had become so great – mainly through accidents – that the strength had been almost halved.

'At the end of August 1944 the name Fighter Interception Unit was dropped, and the unit assumed the identity of No 501 Squadron. The day fighter pilots of the original 501 Squadron were allocated to 2nd TAF units, and so the County of Gloucester Squadron began an entirely new phase, operating solely at night in pursuit of its task. We were left in no doubt about the importance of the job we had to do. Squadron Leader Berry was called to HQ 11 Group and was given specific high-level instructions, which he passed on to us. He had been informed that Winston Churchill had taken a special interest in the new Tempest night-fighter set-up, and that the Prime Minister had issued the following directive:

"So great is the threat, especially at night, of the new V-1 menace, and the possibilities in terms of morale so dire, that No 501 Squadron must consider itself expendable. The Squadron will continue to fly, though there may be little chance of interception, however bad the weather."

'So, night after night, through September and onwards, patrols of 501 Squadron would take off in weather so bad that it sometimes grounded other squadrons during daylight hours. This, together with the fact that our own anti-aircraft gunners now had the benefit of radar gunlaying apparatus and proximity fuses, made our night operations decidedly hairy. Squadron Leader Joe Berry was one of our early casualties; he had been in the anti flying-bomb business a long time, and by the time of his death his score stood officially at 61 destroyed, plus another which he shared with two more pilots. Berry was lost about the middle of September, at the same time as Flight Lieutenant Snowy Bond, a New Zealand pilot, and another New Zealander whose name I forget. Both had been members of the old 501 Squadron in the pre-Tempest days. [*Author: according to records, Squadron Leader Berry was shot down by flak over Veendam, Holland, on 2 October 1944*].

'The Squadron was taken over by Squadron Leader Parker-Rees, who came to us from No 96 Squadron and who was an experienced Mosquito night fighter pilot. At this time No 501 Squadron had seventeen pilots on strength, drawn from a wide area of operational experience.

'Midway through September 1944 No 501 Squadron was moved from Manston to Bradwell Bay, sixteen miles north-east of Southend in Essex, and continued its regular anti-*Diver* patrols from this new location. By the time of the move to Bradwell Bay our defences had become rather more organised; strong anti-aircraft forces had been mustered in the south-east corner of the country, and with their new equipment were beginning to take a substantial toll of the V-1s. We were all "zoned", and No 501 Squadron was responsible for an area over the Thames estuary between Southend and London. Fortunately, our patrol height was somewhat higher than the altitude setting of the anti-aircraft shells. It was also considerably higher than the normal height at which the V-1s flew. As I recall, they flew at between 500 and 1,000 feet. As you may well understand, this was not a comfortable height from which to deliver attacks on anything at night, especially something streaming a long, fiery tail and liable to explode in your face.

'We were equipped with a ground proximity warning device which was supposed to illuminate a red lamp in the cockpit at 500 feet above ground level. I don't think it ever worked.

'From this point on it was the anti-aircraft defences that got the majority of the V-1 intruders. Our task was to try to intercept those that got through the anti-aircraft net. The period of night fighting extended from August 1944 to the end of March 1945, and towards the end of this period No 501 Squadron was moved from Bradwell Bay to Hunsdon, in Hertfordshire, just north of London. During the whole of this period I managed to down two V-1s. I had attempted numerous interceptions throughout the winter, but I had always been beaten to the kill by the AA guns. My first V-1 kill was on the night of 29 October, the V-1 falling somewhere in the vicinity of Chelmsford. My aircraft was Tempest SD-V.

'My second V-1 was shot down on the night of 26 March 1945, when I was operating out of Hunsdon. It was an interesting kill, both for myself and for 501 Squadron. The V-1 crashed and exploded near North Weald, and as far as I can ascertain this was the last success scored against an enemy intruder over Britain. The V-1 offensive ended on 29 March, when a V-1 came down at Datchworth, near Hatfield, but this was not intercepted. At the end of March 1945 No 501 Squadron's role as a night fighter squadron came to an end.

'One point about the Tempest and the flying bomb. As I mentioned earlier, the V-1 was programmed to come across at low level, usually at between 500 feet and 1,000 feet and at high speed, but this was variable. According to official sources, the V-1's average penetration speed was 400 mph, but the second one I caught must have been doing close on 500. From 5,000 feet plus, my Tempest picked up some 580 mph IAS before I was able to catch up with it and destroy it.'

Officially, No 501 Squadron was credited with the destruction of more than 100 V-1s during that dark and freezing winter, but Flight Lieutenant Grottick believes this figure to be exaggerated. 'It was the anti-aircraft that got most of the flying bombs penetrating at night. All that was left for us to do was to try to catch the remnant that got through this first line of defence.'

Nevertheless, there is no disputing the courage and skill of the pilots, who launched themselves into the darkness night after night, in single-engined aircraft that were ill-equipped for the job they had to do, with the knowledge that they were officially expendable.

The Mosquito squadrons also began to take losses in the later phases of the campaign against the V-1. In September 1944, with their bases in the Pas de Calais overrun by the Allied advance, the enemy began flying bomb attacks on London and other UK targets, such as Portsmouth and Southampton, with V-1s air-launched from He 111s of KG53. Later in September air launches were made against east coast targets from positions off the Dutch coast. Catching the Heinkel launchers was very difficult, for they flew slowly at low level, and several Mosquitoes were lost to return fire, or because they stalled at low speed while trying to intercept. In an attempt to improve interception rates, a radar picket ship, the frigate HMS *Caicos*, and a specially-equipped radar Wellington of the Fighter Interception Unit were used to direct the Mosquitoes, which patrolled over the sea at about 4,000 feet between Britain and Holland. These operations continued until 14 January 1945, by which time KG53 had lost seventy-seven aircraft, forty-one of them on operations.

CHAPTER EIGHT

NORTH AFRICA, MALTA AND ITALY

Hurricane Mk IIc of No 94 Squadron at Gamil, May 1942. Note the plate just forward of the cockpit, fitted to protect the pilot's night vision from the glare of the exhaust. (Philip Jarrett)

Germany's entry into the North African theatre in April 1941 brought with it the threat of day and night bombing raids on the Suez Canal Zone, and in May No 94 Squadron, which had just exchanged its Gloster Gladiators for Hurricanes at Ismailia, was assigned to air defence duties, in which role it operated until relieved by No 213 Squadron in December. Both squadrons were equipped with Hurricane Is, which were not fitted with tropical filters and were deemed usuitable for desert operations. The Hurricanes' role as night fighters in the Middle East was short-lived, however, for in December 1941 No 89 Squadron arrived at Abu Sueir with Beaufighter Mk Is, and in May 1941 No 46 Squadron began reforming as a night fighter unit at Idku, initially using some of 89 Squadron's aircraft. These two squadrons remained responsible for the night defence of the Canal

Zone, and for protection of coastal shipping, throughout 1942, providing occasional detachments to Malta and, in 1943, carrying out intruder patrols over the Greek islands and Sicily.

Number 89 Squadron left for Ceylon in October 1943, while No 46 Squadron continued to provide air defence detachments around the eastern Mediterranean. In December 1942, meanwhile, another RAF Beaufighter night fighter squadron, No 153, had arrived in North Africa; based at Maison Blanche in Algeria, its task was to protect the North African ports following the Allied invasion of November 1942 (Operation *Torch*). In March 1943 No 108 Squadron, which had been operating in the night-bombing role from various locations in North Africa, reformed as a night fighter unit at Shandur with Beaufighter VIs, flying night patrols over Egypt and Libya before moving

The Mosquito Mk XIX, with Merlin 25 engines, equipped Nos 600 and 255 Squadrons in Italy from September 1944. (Philip Jarrett)

to Malta in June. Early in 1943 four USAAF night fighter units also arrived in North Africa; these were the 414th, 415th, 416th and 417th FS, whose crews had trained with RAF units in the UK. All four were armed with the Beaufighter VIF; they subsequently moved to Sicily and Italy, and were the only night fighter units operating with the United States Twelfth Air Force.

In December 1942 No 23 Squadron's Mosquitoes arrived at Luqa, Malta, from the UK, having flown there via Gibraltar, and at once began intruder operations over Sicily, with enemy airfields the principal targets. The squadron also carried out night operations against retreating enemy columns in the Tripoli area, and in February 1943 it extended its area of operations to southern Italy. By May 1943 it had destroyed fifteen enemy aircraft, with three probables and eleven damaged, and had also carried out 200 successful attacks on trains. The squadron flew 233 sorties in May, of which 175 were intruder patrols, claiming six enemy aircraft destroyed and sixty-five locomotives attacked, but at the cost of seven Mosquitoes lost. By July, now equipped with Mosquito Mk VI fighter-bombers fitted with drop tanks, the squadron was ranging as far afield as Rome and Foggia, but enemy aircraft

were encountered only occasionally; one exception was an Me 210, shot down by Flight Sergeant P. Rudd in the Taranto area on 26 July.

As mentioned earlier, No 108 Squadron brought its Beaufighter VIs to Luqa in June 1943, and in the following month it was joined by a detachment of six Mosquito Mk XIIs belonging to No 256 Squadron. Both squadrons operated intensively in support of the Allied invasion of Sicily, No 256 claiming sixteen enemy aircraft in a single week, its victims including Ju 88s, He 111s and Cant 1007s. The remainder of the squadron, armed with Mosquito Mk XIIIs, arrived in November. Its commitment was to defend Malta by day and night, with four and three crews repectively on standby during each period. Number 108 Squadron, in the meantime, soldiered on with its ageing Beaufighters, and the arrival of its first Mosquitoes in February 1944 was greeted with euphoria. It was short-lived; the new Mosquitoes were flown by crews drawn from 256 Squadron, and No 108 continued to fly Beaufighters until 5 April, when it flew its first Mosquito patrol. From then until July the squadron flew intruder patrols from Hal Far, using a mixture of Beaufighters and Mosquitoes; the Beaufighters then went to Libya for intruder operations over

Greece and the Aegean, while the Mosquitoes were assigned to No 256 Squadron. The squadron personnel, to say the least, were not happy.

Number 23 Squadron, meanwhile, had moved up to Sicily in October 1943, detachments going to Sigonella and Gerbini Main. In November a detachment moved to Pomigliano, on the Italian peninsula, which was heavily attacked by fifteen FW 190s on the 30th, luckily without causing any aircraft losses. Further detachments went to Alghero, Sardinia, in December 1943, so that the Mosquitoes could now range in an arc from Toulon to Rome. By the end of January 1944 No 23 Squadron had destroyed thirty-three enemy aircraft in air combat and thirty-nine on the ground, as well as attacking 331 locomotives. The squadron flew its last intruder sorties on 2 May, returning to the UK soon afterwards for bomber support operations with No 100 Group.

During 1944 No 256 Squadron, still based on Luqa in Malta, regularly deployed its Mosquitoes forward to Catania in Sicily, from where it flew night patrols over Allied convoys. In March a detachment moved up to Pomigliano to cover the Anzio beachhead, and in April there was a deployment to Algiers, from where patrols were flown over resupply convoys entering the Mediterranean. During these activities the squadron claimed three Ju 88s destroyed and one damaged. Returning to Italy, No 256 Squadron installed itself at Foggia in September 1944 to begin intruder patrols over Greece and the Balkans, and on 4 October two Ju 52s and an He 111 were shot down near Salonika.

The same month saw the arrival of the first Mosquito NF30s in the Middle East, and in December two Beaufighter squadrons, Nos 600 and 255, began rearming with Mk XIXs at Cesenatico and Foggia. Number 255 Squadron's main task was to provide night support for No 232 (Boston) Wing, which had been suffering losses, but there was no contact with enemy aircraft until the night 22/23 March, when a Ju 188 was destroyed.

With the war in Europe over, many Mosquito NFXIXs were transferred from Italy to India, where they replaced the Beaufighter VIs of Nos 89 and 176 Squadrons at Baigachi. Neither squadron saw action with their new aircraft before the end of hostilities.

CHAPTER NINE

THE NIGHT DEFENCE OF GERMANY, 1943–45

By the spring of 1943, General Josef Kammhuber had five *Geschwader* and 400 twin-engined fighters under his command on bases stretching from Holland to the Mediterranean. However, he was the first to realise that 400 night fighters were not enough to counter the great armadas of four-engined bombers that were beginning to make deeper inroads into Germany night after night, and he consequently proposed a major extension of the *Himmelbett* air defence system, with eighteen night fighter *Geschwader* covering the whole of Germany. The aircraft would be fitted with improved AI equipment and the ground radar network would also be modernised.

Kammhuber pushed relentlessly for the expansion of his night fighter force, and it was his undoing. Nothing could convince Hitler that the *Luftwaffe's* night fighters were not already destroying enough enemy bombers to cripple the RAF's night offensive. Kammhuber rapidly began to fall from favour, and his cause was not helped when, during a series of heavy attacks on Hamburg in July 1943, Bomber Command rendered the *Himmelbett* radar system virtually impotent by the use of 'Window', bundles of tinfoil strips cut to the wavelength of the enemy warning radar and dropped from attacking aircraft to confuse the defences.

The paralysing of the *Himmelbett* system led to the evolution of new tactics, stemming from a

A Halifax bomber silhouetted against the fires of a German city – the view a Wilde Sau *pilot would see.* (Author)

proposal made by a Colonel von Lossberg of the General Staff. He recommended that night fighters be released from the confines of the *Himmelbett* zones, where their movements were too restricted and susceptible to radar jamming, and instead mix freely with the bomber stream, the pilots making visual attacks. The idea was approved, and it was decided as a first step to increase the strength of *Jagdgeschwader* 300, formed a month earlier under the command of Major Hajo Hermann, himself a fighter ace. This was the pioneer *Wilde Sau* (Wild Boar) unit; equipped with single-engined fighters, its task was to patrol directly over German targets, the pilots endeavouring to pick out enemy bombers in the glare of searchlights and fires.

The idea was quickly adopted by other night fighter units, including NJG1, and it achieved considerable success – although at great risk to the attacking fighters, which had to contend with German flak as well as defensive fire from the RAF bombers. The following combat report, one of the few to survive the wholesale destruction of *Luftwaffe* records that took place in the final days of the war, was made by *Leutnant* Musset of 5/NJG1. His observer was *Gefreiter* Hafner.

> 'At 2347 hours on 17.8.43 I took off from Berlin on a *Wilde Sau* operation. From the Berlin area I observed enemy activity to the north. I promptly flew in that direction and positioned myself at a height of 4,300 metres over the enemy's target, Peenemünde [*Germany's secret rocket weapons research establishment, hit by 597 heavy bombers that night – author*]. Against the glow of the burning target I saw from above numerous enemy aircraft flying over it in close formations of seven or eight.
>
> 'I went down and placed myself at 3,400 metres behind one enemy formation. At 0142 I attacked one of the enemy with two bursts of fire from directly astern, registering good strikes on the port inboard engine, which at once caught fire. E/A (enemy aircraft) tipped over to its left and went down. Enemy counter-fire from rear gunner was ineffective. Owing to an immediate second engagement I could only follow E/A's descent on fire as far as a layer of mist.
>
> 'I make four claims, as follows:
>
> 1. Attack at 0145 on a four-engined E/A at 2,600 metres from astern and range 30–40 metres. E/A at once burned brightly in both wings and fuselage. I observed it until it crashed in flames at 0147.
> 2. At 0150 I was in position to attack another E/A from slightly above, starboard astern and range 60–70 metres. Strikes were seen in starboard wing, and E/A blew up. I observed burning fragments hit the ground at 0152.
> 3. At 0157 I attacked another four-engined E/A at 1,830 metres from 100 metres astern. Burning brightly in both wings and fuselage it went into a vertical dive. After its crash I saw the wreckage burning at 0158. Heavy counter-fire from rear gunner scored hits in both wings of our own aircraft.
> 4. At 0159 I was ready to attack again. E/A took strong evasive action by weaving. While it was in a left-hand turn, however, I got in a burst from port astern and range 40–50 metres, which set the port wing on fire. E/A plunged to the ground burning brightly, and I observed the crash at 0201. Enemy counter-fire from rear gunner was ineffective.
>
> 'A few minutes later I attacked another E/A which took violent evasive action by weaving. On the first attack my cannon went out of action owing to burst barrels. I then made three further attacks with MG and observed good strikes on the starboard wing without, however, setting it on fire. Owing to heavy counter-fire from enemy rear gunner I suffered hits in my own port engine. At the same time I came under heavy fire from aircraft on the starboard beam, which wounded radio operator in the left shoulder and set my Me 110's port engine on fire. Thereupon I broke off the action, cut my engine and flew westwards away from the target area. No radio contact with the ground could be established, and ES signals were also unavailing. As I was constantly losing height, at 1,800 metres I gave the order to bale out.
>
> 'As I did so I struck the tail unit with both legs, thereby breaking my right thigh and left shin-bone. After normal landings by parachute my observer and I were taken to the reserve military hospital at Güstrow.
>
> 'At 0250 the Me 110 crashed on the northern perimeter of Güstrow.'

Four heavy bombers, each with a crew of seven, destroyed in fifteen minutes, together with one probably destroyed and one damaged! And such engagements were by no means uncommon in the night battle over Germany. That night, forty RAF bombers failed to return from Peenemünde. The loss would undoubtedly have been higher, had it not been for a diversionary effort by a small force of Mosquitoes, which dropped flares over Berlin and duped the defences into believing that this was the objective. The result was that 148 *Wilde Sau* fighters patrolled over the capital for the best part of an hour without sighting a single enemy aircraft.

While *Wilde Sau* operations continued, Telefunken had been hard at work developing a new AI radar that would not be susceptible to *Window* jamming. In October 1943 the night fighter units began to receive the new *Lichtenstein* SN2 AI radar, which was free from both electronic and *Window* jamming. It had a maximum range of four miles and a minimum range of 450 yards, and it was not long before some night fighter crews began to register a formidable number of successes with its help. In the autumn of 1943 two more homing devices were also developed for use by night fighters, the *Naxos* Z and the *Flensburg*. The former enabled the fighters to

This and next page: Lichtenstein-*equipped Ju 88. The drag caused by the 'toasting fork' aerial array knocked several knots off the aircraft's speed.* (Philip Jarrett)

home on transmissions from the RAF's H2S blind bombing radar, and the latter was designed to lock on to radiations from the 'Monica' tail warning radar carried by the bombers.

In the summer of 1943 the German night fighters also began to receive a new type of armament, which was to prove extremely effective. Devised by an NCO armourer named Paul Mahle and known as *Schräge Musik* (Slanting Music), it involved the mounting of two 20 mm cannon, their muzzles pointing upwards at a fixed angle, on a wooden platform in the upper fuselage of a night fighter. This arrangement enabled the fighter to take advantage of a bomber's blind spot and attack it from directly below with the aid of a reflector sight mounted in the cockpit roof.

Schräge Musik was used for the first time on 17/18 August 1943, when two crews of 2/NJG5 destroyed six RAF bombers in the space of half an hour. The German airmen reported that the Halifaxes and Lancasters were extremely vulnerable to this form of attack. The large area of their wings was impossible to miss, and since the wings contained the fuel tanks a relatively short burst was usually enough to set a bomber on fire. Between the night of the Peenemünde raid and 2 October, the crews of 2/NJG5 scored eighteen victories with the aid of *Schräge Musik* for no loss to themselves.

It was a terrible irony that the original specification for the Lancaster and Halifax had included a

ventral gun turret; it had been dispensed with at an early design stage to permit the carriage of a greater bomb load. As a result of losses caused by fighter attacks from below, some bombers – notably in No 6 (RCAF) Group – were locally modified to incorporate a lower fuselage hatch through which a 0.50 in machine-gun could be operated by a crew member.

Despite the problems of equipment and organisation that handicapped the German night fighter force, its success rate reached an unprecedented peak in the spring of 1944. In the course of three big air battles over darkened Germany, Bomber Command suffered crippling losses. On 19/20 February, seventy-eight out of a force of 823 heavy bombers despatched to attack Leipzig failed to

This Lichtenstein-*equipped Ju 88G-1 of 7/NJG2 landed in error at Woodbridge on 13 July 1944. It was extensively tested by the RAF.* (Philip Jarrett)

return; seventy-two more were destroyed during an assault on Berlin on 24/25 March; and then, five nights later, came the most catastrophic loss of all, and the greatest triumph for the night fighters.

At nightfall on 30 March 1944, 795 heavy bombers set out from their English bases to attack the important industrial centre and railway junction of Nuremberg. The night was cloudless and calm, and across a great arc of Europe stretching across Holland, Belgium, northern France and north-west Germany the *Luftwaffe* night fighter crews were at cockpit readiness. At 22.00 reports began to come in of small-scale attacks by Mosquitoes on several airfields in Holland and of minelaying operations over the North Sea, but the GOC I Fighter Corps, *Generalmajor* Josef Schmid, realised that these were simply diversions and kept his fighters on the ground. Then, at 22.30, the German coastal radar stations detected a major raid building up on the other side of the English Channel, and a few minutes later the bomber stream was reported to be heading south-eastwards towards Belgium. At 22.30 Schmid finally ordered his fighters into the air.

This time, instead of carrying out the normal procedure and making several changes of course to confuse the defences, the bomber stream continued due east for 150 miles after making landfall on the enemy coast, and the night fighters had no difficulty in locating their targets. The route to Nuremberg was marked by a series of fiery beacons as one heavy bomber after another fell burning from the sky. From all over Germany the night fighter *Gruppen* converged on the bomber stream, and several pilots scored multiple kills in the battle that developed. The greatest success was achieved by *Oberleutnant* Martin Becker of 1/NJG6, who destroyed six

Halifaxes in thirty minutes, between 00.20 and 00.50 hours. Nor was that all; after landing to refuel and rearm, Becker took off again in his Me 110 and shot down a seventh Halifax as it was on its homeward flight.

Other pilots who achieved notable successes that night were *Oberleutnant* Helmut Schulte of 2/NJG5, who destroyed four heavy bombers; *Leutnant* Wilhelm Seuss of 4/NJG5, who also shot down four; and *Oberleutnant* Martin Drewes of 2/NJG1, who destroyed three.

For RAF Bomber Command, the cost of the Nuremberg raid was stupendous: ninety-five bombers failed to return and seventy-one were damaged. The loss – 11.8 per cent of the attacking force – was the highest ever sustained by the Command. It was the greatest victory achieved by the German night fighter force during the war, but it was also its last. One by one, the leading German night fighter crews were swallowed up in the cauldron of the air war as 1944 wore on; the *Luftwaffe's* night fighter resources dwindled steadily through attrition in combat and through Allied bombing. For example, 465 Me 110s, earmarked for night fighting, were destroyed by Allied bombing in February 1944 alone.

In the first half of 1943, *General* Kammhuber had pressed strongly for the production of new twin-engined types designed specifically for night fighting. At the forefront of these was the He 219 *Uhu* (Owl), the prototype of which had flown in November 1942 after months of delay caused by a lack of interest on the part of the German Air Ministry. By April 1943 300 examples had been ordered; Kammhuber wanted 2,000, but in the event only 294 were built before the end of the war. Formidably armed with six 20 mm cannon and

The Focke-Wulf Ta 154 (V3 pictured here) might have been a valuable addition to the German night fighter force, but it suffered serious structural bonding problems. (Philip Jarrett)

equipped with the latest AI radar, the He 219 would certainly have torn great gaps in Bomber Command's ranks had it been available in quantity. It also had a performance comparable to that of the Mosquito, which other German night fighters did not, and therefore could have fought the RAF's intruders on equal terms.

Admittedly, the He 219 suffered from a series of technical troubles in its early development career, but what it might have achieved in action was ably demonstrated on 11/12 June 1943 by *Major* Werner Streib of 1/NJG1. Flying a pre-production He 219 on operational trials from Venlo, he infiltrated an RAF bomber stream heading for Berlin and shot down five Lancasters in half an hour. The only sour note for Streib sounded when the flaps of the He 219 refused to function and the aircraft overran the runway on landing, breaking into three pieces. Streib and his observer escaped without injury.

Squadron Leader Lewis Brandon and Flight Lieutenant James Benson encountered one of these formidable aircraft on 5/6 January 1945, over northern Germany. They had been following a contact which, disappointingly, turned out to be a Lancaster bomber when Brandon suddenly picked up another trace on his radar screen. Whatever the strange aircraft was, it proved very hard to catch, climbing fast towards Hannover. Benson finally caught it at a range of half a mile over the burning city and identified it as an He 219, easily recognisable because of its twin fins and array of radar aerials.

Benson crept up behind the enemy aircraft and

opened fire at 200 yards, hitting the Heinkel's engines. Large pieces broke off and it went down in a steep dive, with the Mosquito following. At 6,000 feet the enemy night fighter entered a steep climb up to 12,000 feet, where it heeled over and dived almost vertically into the ground. The Mosquito crew saw it blow up. Later, it was learned that the He 219 was fitted with ejection seats, the first aircraft in the world to use them. From the aircraft's erratic behaviour after its initial dive, it seemed likely that the crew of this particular He 219 had ejected from their stricken machine.

Another promising night fighter design that fell by the wayside was the Focke-Wulf Ta 154 Moskito. The Ta 154 was of mixed metal and wood construction, and featured a tricycle undercarriage, with large-diameter tyres to facilitate take-offs from unprepared strips. Powered by two Junkers Jumo 211F engines, the Ta 154 carried a crew of two (pilot and radio/radar operator). Armament comprised two forward-firing 30 mm and two 20 mm cannon, with a single 30 mm cannon mounted obliquely in the rear fuselage. The prototype Ta 154V-1 flew in July 1943 and the type was ordered into production in November, but there were continual delays and in June 1944 the first two production Ta 154A-1s were accidentally destroyed – one when it fell apart because faulty glue had been used in its assembly and the other when its flaps broke away on a landing approach – and as a result the production order was cancelled. Seven more production Ta 154A-1s were completed, however, and these were used operationally for a while by

Above and below: *Messerschmitt Me 262B-1a/U1 night fighter with SN-2* Lichtenstein *AI. This is a captured example, bearing a British serial number. Note the under-fuselage drop tanks. The figure standing beside the aircraft in the second photograph gives a good impression of the Me 262's size.* (Philip Jarrett)

1/NJG3 at Stade and by NJGr10. There is no record of their combat achievements, if indeed there were any.

The Me 110 and the Ju 88 consequently formed the backbone of the German night fighter force. The Ju 88 was the real mainstay; 4,200 were produced as night fighters or converted to the night fighter role. But apart from the He 219, the Germans never fielded a purpose-built night fighter.

A few weeks before the end of hostilities the Germans belatedly realised the potential of the jet-propelled Me 262 as a night fighter, and a single night fighter *Staffel*, 10/NJG11, equipped with the jets in March 1945. On the night 30/31 March, the unit's commander, *Leutnant* Welter, destroyed four

Opposite and this page: *The battle against the German night fighters was never-ending, and the Telecommunications Research Establishment at Malvern was at the heart of it. These photographs show a variety of tail warning equipment under test on B-17 Fortress and Wellington aircraft.* (RRE)

Mosquitoes on the approaches to Berlin – the biggest individual claim against these fast, twin-engined light bombers. The next morning, Halifaxes of No 6 (RCAF) Group, operating over Hamburg by daylight without fighter cover, were attacked by thirty Me 262s of 10/NJG11 and eight of the bombers were shot down.

Many factors combined to bring about the defeat of the German night fighters, not least of which was a continual shortage of suitable aircraft. There was also the priority given to anti-aircraft guns and ammunition at the expense of fighter production, even though fighters were two or three times more effective in terms of kills than anti-aircraft artillery. It is a quite astonishing fact that the amount of aluminium used in manufacturing flak shell fuses throughout the war would have enabled the German aircraft industry to produce 40,000 more fighters, in addition to the 54,000 actually built.

But perhaps the biggest single factor was radio countermeasures (RCM), a field in which the British enjoyed an undisputed lead in their ongoing night offensive against Germany. Thanks to the 'Y' Service, *Ultra* and the various agencies that monitored German signals traffic, the threat presented by the German controlled night fighter system to the RAF's night bombing offensive was well known by the beginning of 1942, and much had been deduced about its operational methods. More knowledge was added in February 1942, when one of the system's key components, a *Wurzburg* precision GCI radar, was captured in a commando raid on Bruneval, near Le Havre, and by May 1942 an almost complete and very accurate picture of enemy GCI fighter control had been built up. At the same time, the loss rate suffered on bombing operations was steadily increasing, and there was no doubt that this was due to the large-scale introduction of radar-assisted control of both AA guns and fighters.

The value of radar countermeasures was not in doubt. The development of airborne jamming equipment had been started in late 1941 and was still in progress. One highly effective countermeasure – *Window* – had already been developed, but its use was not yet authorised on the grounds that Britain was still too vulnerable to air attack for the RAF to initiate a jamming war.

By the autumn of 1942, however, losses had become so severe that a continued embargo on radar countermeasures could no longer be justified, and on 6 October a meeting was held at HQ Bomber Command to consider their adoption. The first recommendation was that the bombers' IFF (Identification Friend/Foe) sets be modified to operate on the frequency (120–130 mc/s) of the *Freya* radars so that some jamming could be effected. It was realised that this countermeasure,

called *Shiver*, would not achieve much success, so the use of a second radar countermeasure was authorised. This was *Mandrel*, a radar jammer developed at the Wembley laboratories of the General Electric Company. It operated in the 120–130 mc/s band, and two aircraft per squadron were to be fitted with it. Its object was to reduce the range at which the *Freya* sets could identify and plot incoming bombers from 100 to about twenty-five miles. Two *Mandrel* ground stations, at Dover and Hastings, would also be brought into use to supplement the airborne equipment.

Steps were also taken to disrupt the vital radio communications link between the night fighters and their ground controllers. This was done by modulating the bombers' transmitters with noise produced by a microphone situated inside the aircraft. Each wireless operator was briefed to search a bank of 150 kc/s between 3 and 6 mc/s and to transmit on the frequency of any German R/T which he heard. This countermeasure, called *Tinsel*, and *Mandrel* were both introduced operationally in December 1942, and a squadron of Boulton Paul Defiants (No 515 Squadron) was also equipped with *Mandrel* and given the task of patrolling fifty miles off the enemy coast.

The effect of *Mandrel* was found to be less than had been hoped, mainly because the enemy extended the frequency range of the *Freya* from 120–130 mc/s to 120–150 mc/s in an effort to minimise the effect of jamming. He also developed a device called *Freya-Halbe*, which enabled night fighters to home on to the jamming aircraft, with the result that losses among the *Mandrel*-equipped bombers were high. It was never possible to raise the *Mandrel* barrage to the desired intensity, and although one estimate suggested that a force of 600 *Mandrel*-equipped aircraft would produce the required result, it was never possible, because of a shortage of equipment, to have more than 200 aircraft fitted with the device at any one time.

A greater success was achieved by *Tinsel*, and in April 1943 the 'Y' Service reported that the Germans were making increasing use of VHF radio communications, which operated between 38 and 42 mc/s and was therefore immune to this countermeasure. Another jamming device, *Ground Cigar*, was set up at Sizewell in Suffolk to deal with the new fighter frequency, but it suffered from a lack of range, with a coverage of only 140 miles from the ground station, and it also disrupted the 'Y' Service's VHF traffic. An airborne version was the obvious answer, and development of one – *Airborne Cigar*, more commonly called ABC – was set in motion.

All the frequencies on which the various German ground–air components of the German air defence system operated, could be monitored and identified

Jostle *noise jamming equipment installed in a Short Stirling.* (RRE)

from the United Kingdom, but the short-range airborne interception radars used by the German night fighters presented a different problem. The first German AI radar, the *Lichtenstein* BC, became operational early in 1942; it operated in the 490 mc/s band and had a maximum range of about two miles.

In July 1942, the 'Y' Service picked up indications that the German night fighters operating over Holland were using an airborne detection device referred to as *Emil*, but its exact nature could not be ascertained. In an attempt to gather more information, a special duties unit, No 1474 Flight, was formed, and its Wellingtons, equipped with radio detection gear, began operations over north-west Europe. Seventeen sorties were flown without result; then, on 3/4 December 1942, the radio operator of an eighteenth Wellington picked up weak signals at 04.30, possibly from German AI radar, on 487 mc/s. The signal strength increased rapidly, and the crew knew that an enemy fighter was locked on to them.

A few moments later the Wellington was heavily attacked by a Ju 88. The captain of the British aircraft, Pilot Officer Paulton, took evasive action and his rear gunner returned the fire. The specialist radio operator, Pilot Officer Jordan, was badly wounded by the night fighter's first burst of fire; he nevertheless went on transmitting information about the enemy radar signals back to base for some minutes before he collapsed. The Ju 88 finally broke off the attack when Paulton took the Wellington down in a long dive from 14,000 to 500 feet. The bomber was severely damaged; both its throttles were jammed, its gun turrets were out of action and most of its instruments had been smashed by shell splinters. As the aircraft limped homewards the second specialist wireless operator, Flight Sergeant Bigoray, continued to transmit data, although he was wounded in both legs. The Wellington ditched 200 yards off the British coast and the crew was rescued. For their part in the mission, Pilot Officer Jordan received the DSO, the pilot was awarded the DFC and Flight Sergeant Bigoray the DFM.

The electronic surveillance missions flown by No

Window, *seen here being manufactured, was – and still is – a very effective anti-radar weapon.* (Author)

1474 Flight were the first ever of their kind, and led to the development of a jamming device called *Ground Grocer*. This covered only a small area of Holland and Belgium and was of limited value. Of much greater importance was the development by the Telecommunications Research Establishment of *Serrate*, described earlier. However, there was no escaping the fact that in the autumn of 1943 Bomber Command's loss rate had once again risen to eighty per cent of the level it had reached prior to the introduction of *Window*, and furthermore British Intelligence was aware that the German night fighter units had begun to equip with the new FUG 220 *Lichtenstein* SN-2 AI radar, developed by Telefunken and resistant to both *Window* and the jamming equipment then in use. In the autumn of 1943 two more homing devices were also developed for use by night fighters, the FUG 350 *Naxos* Z and the FUG 227 *Flensburg*.

In the early months of 1944 the Allies knew very little about this new equipment, and went to great lengths to gather reliable intelligence data on it. Many perilous sorties were flown by No 192 Squadron – the former 1474 Flight – operating out of Gransden Lodge in Cambridgeshire with a mixture of Wellingtons, Halifaxes and Mosquitoes, but with no result. The Mosquitoes alone flew fifty-

five sorties in the first three months of the year, five to the Berlin area.

The Germans had unrestricted use of *Lichtenstein* SN-2 for a full six months, during which Bomber Command suffered appalling losses. The only clues to the nature of the new equipment were some signals which had been picked up in the 160 mc/s range and which might have emanated from an AI radar, and a gun-camera photograph, taken by an American fighter, which showed a Ju 88 on the ground featuring a novel type of aerial array. The dimensions of the array, as deduced from the poor-quality photograph, suggested a frequency of around 100 mc/s, which was thought to be too low to produce reliable results. On the assumption – incorrect, as it turned out – that 160 mc/s was likely to be the frequency of the new enemy AI radar, a new type of *Window* called Type Y was produced.

It was never used operationally, for on 12/13 July 1944 a Junkers Ju 88G night fighter made a serious navigational error and landed at Woodbridge in Suffolk. The aircraft was equipped with both SN-2 AI radar and the *Flensburg* homing device, which were quickly subjected to a thorough evaluation by the Telecommunications Research Establishment. The examination showed that the SN-2 worked on a frequency of around 90 mc/s, and luckily a countermeasure was already available in the form of *Window* Type MB, which had been devised for use in connection with the D-Day landings and which covered all frequencies between 70 and 200 mc/s. Good stocks were still in hand, and on 23/24 July it was dropped on a normal operation. Almost immediately, bomber losses began to decline.

Several problems were experienced in the creation of No 100 Group's RCM force. The first lay in the choice of a suitable aircraft, which had to be big enough to carry the necessary equipment and able to fly fast and high enough to stand a chance of avoiding night fighters. The aircraft selected eventually was the Boeing B-17 Flying Fortress, which was considered to meet all the requirements. Fourteen B-17Fs were obtained, and necessary modifications were carried out early in 1944 by the Scottish Aviation Company at Prestwick. These included the replacement of the Fortress's chin turret by an H2S blister, the provision of mufflers to screen the exhaust flames and the fitting of the jamming devices in the bomb bay. The aircraft began operations with No 214 Squadron in June 1944. In addition, B-17s of the 803rd Squadron, United States Strategic Air Forces, were also equipped for the jamming role, and this unit was placed under the operational control of No 100 Group.

The RCM devices carried by these aircraft were called *Jostle* and *Piperack*. The first, a high-powered communications jammer, emitted a high-pitched wail and could effectively jam any frequency used by the German fighter controllers; the second, developed from an American RCM kit called *Dina*, designed to reinforce *Mandrel*, covered the 90–110 mc/s frequency used by the German AI radars. A third squadron, No 223, which was equipped with Liberators and which began operations in September 1944, was also equipped with these devices. *Mandrel* operations, which did not require fast, high-flying aircraft since they were usually conducted clear of enemy territory, were flown by the Stirlings of No 199 Squadron and the Halifaxes of No 171, joined at the end of 1944 by the Halifaxes of No 642 Squadron. Meanwhile, No 192 Squadron continued to monitor enemy radio and radar transmissions, and in late 1944 it wasted a lot of effort in searching for the radio signals that were mistakenly thought to guide V-2 rockets.

In their finalised form, the tactics used by No 100 Group's RCM force were as follows. *Mandrel*-equipped aircraft, employed mainly to provide a screen for the main bomber force, would operate in pairs with fourteen miles between them, forming a line positioned some eighty miles from enemy territory. With their *Mandrels* switched on, the orbiting aircraft formed an effective electronic curtain through which the enemy search radars were unable to penetrate. Aircraft equipped with *Jostle* and *Piperack*, on the other hand, flew 4,000 feet above the bomber stream at intervals of ten miles, providing an electronic umbrella to disrupt the German AI radar and voice communications.

The Germans tried desperately to remain a step ahead of Allied countermeasures developments. Early in 1944 they began work on two new types of AI radar, the FUG 218 *Neptun* VR and the FUG 228 *Lichtenstein* SN-3. The former worked in the 163-187 mc/s band, the latter in the 100–112 mc/s band, and the frequencies of both could be altered in the air to make jamming more difficult. Production of the SN-3 had already started when the Allies found an effective means of jamming the German *Freya* ground radar, which worked on the same waveband, so further work on the SN-3 AI set was stopped and production concentrated on *Neptun*. This was first used operationally in February 1945, but the Allies quickly discovered that it was vulnerable to *Window* of the right length and within three weeks effective countermeasures had been devised against it.

CHAPTER TEN

THE FAR EAST AND THE PACIFIC

The night fighter squadrons of RAF Fighter Command had been battling the *Luftwaffe* for more than a year when the Japanese launched their invasion of South-East Asia; and yet, despite all the warnings and all the lessons of experience, when Japanese bombers began intensive night raids on Singapore and Rangoon, there was not a single dedicated night fighter squadron to oppose them. Only one RAF squadron in Malaya, No 27, was equipped with Blenheim IF fighters, and these were assigned to the day fighting role. In the event the matter quickly became academic, for the Blenheims were soon destroyed by air attacks on their airfields, and it was left to the handful of RAF, RAAF and RNZAF single-engined squadrons – all equipped with the totally inadequate Brewster Buffalo – to fight on by day and night until they were eventually overwhelmed.

In Burma the scenario was similar, but here the Japanese Air Force encountered tougher opposition and better equipment. Here, one RAF Buffalo squadron (No 67) fought alongside the experienced pilots of the American Volunteer Group, who, flying Curtiss P-40s, had already been fighting the Japanese in China for some time. Between them, they inflicted substantial losses on the Japanese bomber formations that attacked the Burmese capital, Rangoon, by daylight in December 1941; and when two squadrons of Hurricanes arrived to replace the Buffaloes in January 1942 the enemy switched almost entirely to night attacks.

An early warning system of sorts was devised, relying on a network of ground observers to give warning of the Japanese bombers' approach by telephone. Ten minutes' warning was usually just enough to enable the defending fighters to gain a height advantage over the bombers as they approached their target. After that, the fighter pilots relied on their eyesight, moonlight and searchlights (of which there were very few) to locate the enemy.

War correspondent O.D. Gallagher, an accurate eye-witness to events in Burma (as far as censorship would allow), described a night battle early in 1942, in his book *Retreat in the Far East*, published by Harrap, London, 1942:

'At last two night fighter pilots arrived from Britain. We were in front of the club [the Mingaladon Golf Club – author] on the big lawn, with some twenty Blenheim pilots, observers and gunners. We heard the distant sirens of Rangoon ... We heard the night-fighter take off (the pilot was Squadron Leader Stone, DFC) and begin its sinister, unseen prowling of the sky. The moonlight was brilliant, although there were some high, patchy, still clouds. Indeed, they seemed to add to the brilliance of the moonlight by reflecting it.

'The Japanese night formation arrived with a trembling drone that filled the air. They were at a great height but we spotted them. They circled the airfield once or twice with their customary arrogance, their usual contempt for the feeble defences. Tonight it was a pleasure to see them keep tight formation, supremely ignorant of the single, higher-pitched sound that manoeuvred around them. They could not, of course, hear the Hurricane with its old night fighter pilot in the cockpit. They certainly could not see it, any more than we could. It was perfectly blacked out – not a twinkle of light from its shielded exhausts ...

'A line of red tracer bullets pierced the sky and shot up vertically. Another – the tracers chased each other upwards until they burned out. Seconds later we heard the rat-tat-tat of Stone's guns ... Tracers shot from another point, obviously fired by the gunner of a Japanese bomber. But at that same moment a new line of red tracers poured downward from an invisible source above them. It was Stone, who had drawn their attention to a spot below the formation, then climbed all out above them and caught them unawares ...

'One of the bombers burst into fire and crashed to the ground. An immense flash as it hit, and later a heavy crump ... In the light of the following day they found the bodies and remains of five Japanese around the wreck. That was the first night fighter success from Mingaladon airfield ...'

Whatever limited success the improvised night fighters in Burma may have enjoyed, it was short-lived. The Allied forces were soon in full retreat towards the Indian border, and the air squadrons, decimated by attacks on their airfields, ceased to exist as a fighting force.

The successful campaign by the Japanese in Burma brought their army to within striking distance of the Plain of Bengal and its teeming capital city of Calcutta. But the enemy needed to regroup and strengthen his forces, and the expected invasion of India failed to materialise in 1942. It was not until December that a threat began to develop and, as a preliminary, the Japanese began to send small numbers of bombers over Calcutta in an attempt to panic the civilian population. Initially, Nos 17 and 79 Squadrons were responsible for the air defence of Calcutta; but as most of the air attacks came in at night, they achieved little result. Matters began to improve in January 1943, when No 176 Squadron formed at Dum Dum from a flight of No 89 Squadron, newly arrived from the Middle East with eight Beaufighter Is. These went into action immediately, and in less than a week they destroyed five Japanese bombers at night – three of them falling to one pilot, Flight Sergeant Pring, on 15/16 January 1943. The Japanese bombers, one observer recalled, were 'uncamouflaged and gleaming like silver fish in the moonlight.'

In May 1943 No 176 Squadron formed a second flight, armed with Hurricane IIcs. These were fitted with AI Mk IV, the installation closely following that in the Defiant, and they remained operational until January 1944, when they were replaced by Beaufighter VIs. Meanwhile, a detachment of Beaufighters had been sent to Ceylon in September 1943 to counter Japanese reconnaissance aircraft. In August 1944, after a period operating from advanced bases in Burma, the squadron moved to southern India, returning to the Burma front in June 1945 and converting to Mosquitoes.

At the time of the Japanese attack in December 1941, the United States Army Air Corps, as it then was, had no specialised night fighter. In fact, scant thought had been given to night fighting at all until the late summer of 1940, when Lieutenant-General Delos C. Emmons, Commanding General of GHQ Air Corps, visited Britain and saw at first hand the threat posed by night bombers. As a result of his recommendations, the USAAC drew up preliminary specifications for a night fighter and passed them to the Northrop Company, which at that time was working on a night fighter design on behalf of the British Purchasing Commission in the USA. The design that was taking shape involved a radar-equipped aircraft with a crew of two, heavy armament and long endurance, so that incoming bombers could be intercepted long before they reached their targets.

Before negotiations could begin with the British on construction of a prototype, the USAAC stepped in and virtually commandeered the project, although British involvement was maintained for the time being; the RAF relinquished its interest when the Beaufighter began to prove its worth in the night defence role. In January 1941 Northrop

received a contract for the construction of two prototypes under the designation XP-61. The aircraft would later be called the Black Widow.

In December 1941, however, the first flight of the XP-61 was still several months away, and the USAAF (which it had become in June that year) identified a pressing need for an interim night fighter. The most logical and speedy solution seemed to be to convert the Douglas A-20 bomber to the night fighting role, as the RAF had done with the Boston/Havoc, and sixty such conversions were authorised under the designation P-70. British AI Mk IV radar was installed in the nose, the antenna being mounted in the nose and wings. A ventral armament pack of four 20 mm cannon, with sixty rounds per gun, was fitted in place of the bomb bay. Deliveries of the first sixty aircraft began in April 1942 and were completed in September, most being allocated for training purposes to the 481st Night Fighter Operational Training Group at Orlando, Florida.

As crews became proficient in handling their aircraft and equipment, they were assigned to squadrons and sent overseas. The first P-70 unit to be sent to the Pacific Theatre was the 6th Night Fighter Squadron (NFS), which arrived in Hawaii in September 1942 and left a detachment there before proceeding to Guadalcanal in March 1943. The 421st NFS was sent to New Guinea. Both proved quite incapable of catching the Japanese bombers they were supposed to intercept, prompting Admiral Halsey, concerned about shipping losses caused by night attacks, to request a new night fighter, possibly the Mosquito. The request was denied, and instead five brand-new P-61As were rushed out to the 421st NFS; P-38 Lightnings were also locally modified to two-seat configuration and fitted with an SCR-540 radar mounted in a drop tank, but they were not used operationally. Instead, unmodified P-38Gs and P-38Js were used as night fighters by the 418th and 421st NFS in New Guinea and the 419th NFS on Guadalcanal, and a few successful interceptions were made. Two single-seat P-38Js fitted with APS-4 radar in Australia were used with some success by the 547th NFS, which operated in the Philippines from late 1944.

However, it was not until the Black Widow began to reach the Pacific Theatre in numbers that the USAAF had a really effective night fighter. The 421st NFS was the first to rearm with the new type, operating from Mokmer in New Guinea, and on 7 July 1944 one of its aircraft scored the first P-61 victory in the Southwest Pacific by shooting down a Mitsubishi Ki46 *Dinah* over Japen island.

The 421st, which was joined in the theatre at later dates by the 418th and 547th NFS, moved to Tacloban, Leyte, on 25 October 1944, and on 29

Above and below: *The Northrop P-61 Black Widow proved deadly in night actions over the Pacific.* (Philip Jarrett)

November the Black Widows were ordered to make a night attack on a Japanese convoy in Leyte Gulf. The convoy, consisting of two escort destroyers and a number of smaller vessels, was heading towards Ormoc to land reinforcement troops and supplies. The convoy was duly harassed throughout the night, preventing the landing of its troops, and one of the destroyers was sunk by United States surface forces at daybreak.

In the Central Pacific, the United States Seventh Air Force had three Black Widow squadrons, the 6th, 548th and 549th. In June 1944 seven P-61s of the 6th NFS moved to Aslito airstrip on Saipan, and on 27 June one of its aircraft claimed a Nakajima B5N *Kate* as probably destroyed. There was no doubt about the outcome on 6 July, when two P-61s sent two Mitsubishi G4M *Betty* bombers down in flames. Two more G4Ms were destroyed on 25/26 December by Lieutenant Dale Haberman (pilot) and Lieutenant Raymond Mooney (RO). The combat report tells the story:

'Scrambled from Condor Base then to Coral Base and vectored to the north of the island at altitude of 15,000 ft. Coral Base ordered figure 8 orbits since they had no Bogies in the vicinity but much Snow (fuzzy radar image) was in the area. Contact made with airborne radar at five miles. Control notified ... reported Bogies in vicinity but could give no information. Went into starboard orbit but airborne radar kept picking up Bogie which seemed to be in orbit. Chased Bogie to the north and let down to 9,000 ft when visual contact was made. Opened fire at 1,500 ft and closed to 700 ft. Bogie made violent turns and hits observed to go into wings and fuselage. Bogie was in a slight dive indicating 300 mph. Bogie last seen to roll to port in semblance of Split-S and nose straight down with fires observed coming from the right wing and engine. Visual lost as Bogie was at 6,000 ft still going straight down, apparently out of control.

'At the same time the Radar Observer called for a starboard turn as a second Bogie was out about two miles. Closed fast on second Bogie letting down to 4,500 ft where visual was made at about 2,500 ft. Closed in to 700 ft and opened fire with hits observed to spray the entire ship. Bogie exploded with its debris hitting P-61 with damage to left cowling. Bogie went down in flames and was seen to hit the water ...'

Two more Black Widow squadrons, the 548th and 549th, arrived in the Pacific on 7 and 24 March 1945 respectively, being assigned to the Seventh Air Force on Iwo Jima. The 548th NFS soon moved up to Ie Shima to provide forward air defence and also to carry out night intruder operations over Kyushu, scoring five kills during these operations; the 549th NFS remained on Iwo Jima, sending detachments to Saipan and Guam as required.

There were two Black Widow squadrons in the China–Burma–India (CBI) Theatre. The first was the 426th NFS, which was activated on 1 January 1944 at Hammer Field, California, and arrived at Chengtu, China, under Fourteenth Air Force command on 5 November 1944. It operated from a number of bases thereafter, mostly in the night ground-attack role, as there was virtually no air opposition. The other was the 427th NFS, which

was activated on 1 February 1944 and deployed to Myitkyina, Burma, in December by way of Italy and India. During the next few months, under the command of the Tenth and later the Fourteenth Air Force, the 427th NFS flew seventy-three defensive patrols without encountering a single enemy aircraft and so its aircraft were modified to carry bombs and rockets for intruder operations against Japanese troop concentrations and supply dumps. A detachment at Kunming, China, carried out similar work.

The hardest-worked P-61 squadron in the Pacific, however, remained the 418th, which saw considerable action against enemy intruders from successive bases in New Guinea, the Schouten Islands, Leyte, Mindoro and Okinawa. A combat report by Lieutenant Bertram C. Tompkins, dated 27 January 1945, describes one of its actions. The squadron was then based on Mindoro.

'Approximately 1½ hours after becoming airborne the GCI controller vectored me onto a Bogey approaching from the north-west. Flying Officer Wertin made radar contact with Bogey at 0010 at a distance of six miles and altitude of 10,000 ft on heading of 280 degrees. He directed me to 2,000 ft directly behind and below Bogey and I obtained a visual and identified it as a *Tony* (Kawasaki Ki-61). I closed to 150 ft and fired one short burst. The *Tony* exploded and fell burning into the water approximately twenty miles west of base. No evasive action was used by enemy aircraft.

'Immediately GCI vectored me onto second Bogey, which was twenty miles south-east of me. Flying Officer Wertin made radar contact at six miles and directed me to 3,000 ft directly behind and slightly below the Bogey, where I got a visual. I closed to 300 ft and fired one burst, and enemy aircraft exploded and fell to the water burning. Kill was made approximately five miles west of Mindoro coast. Enemy Aircraft was identified as a *Tony*. Violent evasive action was used.'

Early night fighting in the USN, like its land-based counterpart, was also an improvised business. It had its beginnings in November 1943, when six heavy and five light carriers of the USN's Task Force 50 opened the campaign to capture the Gilbert Islands with a two-day series of strikes on Japanese airfields and installations in support of American landings on Tarawa and Makin Atolls. The Task Force Commander, Rear-Admiral Pownall, was concerned about Japanese night attacks on his ships, and invited ideas on how they might be protected.

Lieutenant-Commander Edward H. (Butch) O'Hare, commanding Air Group 6 on the carrier USS *Enterprise*, and some of his fellow pilots came up with a possible answer. The *Enterprise* had one of the new radar-equipped Grumman TBF-1C

Close-up of the AN/APS-6 radar pod on the starboard wing of a Grumman F6F-3N Hellcat. (Philip Jarrett)

Avengers, and the plan was to form an interception team with this aircraft and two Hellcat fighters. The Hellcats, each of which would be flown by a pilot with night experience, would form up on the Avenger; the formation would be vectored to the vicinity of an enemy contact by the carrier's Fighter Director and the Avenger's radar would then take over, bringing the fighters to within visual range of the target.

The first sortie, on 24/25 November, did not result in any intercepts, but on 26/27 the trio got in amongst a formation of G4M bombers and caused havoc. The Avenger was the aircraft that scored, its pilot and gunner accounting for two of the *Betty*s; the Wildcats also attacked separate targets, with the result that the enemy raid was severely disrupted. 'Butch' O'Hare went missing during this engagement and was never seen again.

From this point onwards *Enterprise* began to specialise in night operations, both offensive and defensive. On 17/18 February 1944, during a heavy assault by US carrier aircraft on the island of Truk, twelve radar-equipped TBF-1Cs of VT-10 from *Enterprise* carried out the first night bombing attack in the history of US carrier aviation, making a low-level raid on the harbour and scoring several direct hits on shipping.

For this campaign, night fighter detachments of

VF(N)-76 and VF(N)-101, armed with F6F-3 Hellcats and F4U-2 Corsairs equipped with AI radar, were assigned to five carriers, and although they were not widely used they were occasionally vectored against enemy night raiders. The first success by a radar-equipped Corsair had in fact been registered on 31 October 1943, when Lieutenant H.D. O'Neil of VF(N)-75 operating from Munda, New Georgia, destroyed a *Betty* during a night attack off Vella Lavella, ground-based fighter direction being provided by Major T.E. Hicks and T/Sgt Gleason of VMF(N)-513.

Eighteen F6F-3E Hellcat night fighters were built, an AN/APS-4 AI radar being fitted into a radome on the starboard wing. The -3N, 150 of which were built, used the improved AN/APS-6 radar. The most numerous of the Hellcat night fighter variants was the F6F-5N, which also had the AN/APS-6; 1,435 were produced in total. Two Royal Navy squadrons, Nos 891 and 892, were equipped with F6F-5Ns under the designation Hellcat IIs.

Like the F6F-3N Hellcat, the Vought F4U-2 Corsair was developed, or rather modified, in response to the need to keep Japanese night intruders at bay. Twelve F4U-2s were converted from F4U-1s drawn from stock and assigned to two units, VF(N)-101 on the USS *Essex* and VF(N)-75

A Grumman Hellcat NFII of the Fleet Air Arm, pictured in March 1945. (Philip Jarrett)

The F4U Corsair night fighter was used by US Marine Corps squadrons in the Pacific, and later in Korea. (Philip Jarrett)

at Munda. Other night fighter versions of the Corsair to serve in the Pacific were the F4U-4E with the AN/APS-4 radar, and the -4N with the AN/APS-6.

On 14 August 1945, the day before the Japanese surrender, a United States Marine Corps night fighter squadron arrived at the Pacific battlefront. This was VMF(N)-533, armed with the potent twin-engined Grumman F7F-2N Tigercat. An aircraft in which the USN had shown little interest, the Tigercat was deployed too late to see action in World War II; its chance would come later, in Korea.

CHAPTER ELEVEN

NIGHT DEFENCE OF JAPAN, 1944–45

On the night of 9/10 March, 1945, B-29s (Superfortresses) of the USAAF's 21st Bomber Command, operating from bases in the Marianas, launched their first major incendiary attack on Japan. The target was Tokyo. At 23.00 a small force of B-29 pathfinder aircraft dropped clusters of 70 lb M47 napalm bombs on an aiming point at the centre of a rectangle measuring three miles by four. During the next three hours the pathfinders were followed by 279 more B-29s, routed individually to the target and stripped of weapons and armour plating to enable them to carry an enhanced load of 500 lb M69 oil-bomb clusters. Each cluster consisted of sixty 6 lb jellied-oil bombs, released from the main canister at 2,000 feet by a time fuse.

The raid and its catastrophic results were witnessed by Major David H. James, a British intelligence officer in the PoW camp at Omori, just over seven miles south of the Imperial Palace in Tokyo. In his book *The Rise and Fall of the Japanese Empire* he subsequently wrote:

'The alert came at 11pm and soon after the alert the air-raid warnings were being sounded all over Tokyo. About midnight there was the drone of aircraft as the first wave came in from the north-east. They were travelling in two streams – from north-east to south-west and from north-west to south-east.

'Ground defence came into action as the first fires appeared at Oji-ku ... almost at the same time as the leading planes crossed overhead. Planes were flying very low. A strong wind was fanning the fires as wave after wave came over and dropped "baskets" of fresh incendiaries over the industrial districts north and east of the Imperial Palace and the factory area to the south-west, bordering Tokyo Bay. Wind direction was north to south. Wave followed wave; they destroyed and then went on into the darkness beyond the flames, their bodies glistening as the beams of searchlights followed them until they were lost to sight in cloud.'

The B-29 bomb aimers in the last waves found their task made difficult by the dense clouds of smoke that billowed over the capital and by the tremendous upcurrents of hot air bursting from the inferno below. There was considerable anti-aircraft fire; nine B-29s were destroyed over the city, and five others were so badly damaged that they had to ditch in the sea; all their crews were picked up safely. Forty-two other bombers sustained varying degrees of flak damage. Seventy-six fighters were sighted and forty attacks were reported, but none of these inflicted any damage.

The 1,667 tons of incendiaries dropped by the B-29s caused a glow in the sky that could be seen 150 miles away. The following morning, photographs brought back by high-flying B-29 reconnaissance aircraft revealed that 15.8 square miles of Tokyo had been razed to the ground, and that twenty-two major industrial targets had been destroyed. Firestorms had swept through a quarter of the city's built-up areas, destroying 267,000 buildings and rendering 1,008,000 people homeless. The official Japanese casualty figures gave the number of dead as 83,793, with 102,000 injured; in fact the total was probably higher. After the war, an official told Allied investigators:

'People were unable to escape. They were found later piled upon the bridges, roads and in the canals, 80,000 dead and twice that many injured. We were instructed to report on actual conditions. Most of us were unable to do this because of horrifying conditions beyond imagination.'

From his vantage point at Omori, Major James observed the horrific consequences of the raid after daybreak.

'All day an acrid smell filled our nostrils ... when the tide lapped our fences it cast up hundreds of charred bodies. We stared through the knot-holes at the men, women and children sprawled in the mud or jammed against the logs from the demolished timber-yards – men, women and children, the remains of human beings left there to rot alongside others who floated in after other raids on the capital.'

The Tokyo raid served to underline the painful inadequacy of the Japanese defences. The early warning system was hopelessly outdated by western standards, and although Tokyo's fire service was the

Above and below: *The Kawasaki Ki-45* Toryu *was a formidable night fighter, having upward-firing cannon mounted in the fuselage, but like all Japanese night fighters it had no AI radar.* (Philip Jarrett)

best in Japan it was completely unable to cope with the outbreak of so many large fires over so wide an area. The result was that the inferno got out of hand within half an hour of the start of the raid. The anti-aircraft batteries were not radar-directed; had it been otherwise, they might have inflicted far more damage on the attackers.

The lack of AI radar also handicapped the Japanese night fighter force. The only operational night fighter available to the Japanese Army was the Kawasaki Ki-45 Toryu, known to the Allies by the codename *Nick*. With its armament of two 20 mm cannon and one 7.92 mm machine-gun it was a formidable enough interceptor, but it was not equipped with AI radar, and although it claimed successes against the B-29 night raiders the burden of night home defence came to be borne increasingly by single-engined day fighter types, using tactics similar to the German *Wilde Sau*.

The ordeal of Japan's cities continued. On 12/13 March it was the turn of Nagoya, the centre of Japan's aircraft industry. Shortly after midnight industrial areas of the city were marked by napalm-carrying B-29 Pathfinders, and during the next three-and-a-half hours 285 bombers unloaded 1,790 tons of incendiaries on and around the aiming points. Nagoya, however, was spared the catastrophe that had engulfed Tokyo. The city's fire brigade had had the foresight to space firebreaks at key points, the water supply was plentiful, and above all there was only a light wind to fan the flames. On this occasion too the bombers released their M69 clusters at intervals of 100 feet instead of 50 feet as had been the case in the Tokyo raid, with the result that the incendiaries had been too widely spaced to build up dangerous firestorms. Nevertheless, although only two square miles of the city were devastated, eighteen major industrial plants were destroyed or badly damaged. All the B-29s returned to base; twenty suffered damage, two of them in fighter attacks.

Two nights later the Superfortresses visited Osaka, the second largest city in Japan. Two hundred and seventy-four B-29s made a radar-directed attack on this target through eight-tenths cloud, razing over eight square miles with 1,732 tons of fire bombs. The enemy death toll was 3,988, with a further 9,000 people injured; while 119 factories and 135,000 houses were wiped out. The B-29 crews reported forty attacks by enemy fighters; two bombers failed to return and thirteen more were damaged.

On 17 March, 21st Bomber Command's effort was switched to Kobe, a vital enemy port. Once again the attack was radar directed. To achieve a better bombing concentration the aiming points were grouped in a confined area and the duration of the raid was reduced. This time, as supplies of M47 napalm and M69 oil bombs were running low in the Marianas, the B-29s carried M17A1s, magnesium thermite incendiary clusters containing 110 four-pound bombs. The Kobe raid was the largest to date, with 307 Superfortresses taking part. In the space of just over two hours they dropped 2,355 tons of incendiaries on the target, totally destroying an area of 2.9 square miles. The Kawasaki shipyards were heavily damaged, while 500 industrial installations were destroyed and 162 damaged. The conflagration destroyed 66,000 houses, making a quarter of a million people homeless; 2,669 were killed and 11,289 injured. Although enemy fighters made ninety-three reported attacks on the raiding force, no B-29s were lost.

On 7 April 1945 21st Bomber Command, now escorted by long-range P-51 Mustang fighters, turned its major effort to a daylight offensive against Japan's principal aero-engine plants. Night attacks continued, however, and on 13/14 April the Americans launched another incendiary attack on Tokyo in which 327 B-29s dropped 2,139 tons of incendiaries, wiping out 11.4 square miles of the city. Vast explosions rocked the city as the fires touched off the contents of munitions factories and arsenals. Two nights later 303 more B-29s bombed Tokyo Baty, Kawasaki and Yokohama, destroying over a quarter of a million buildings.

By mid-May 1945 four B-29 wings (the 58th, 73rd, 313th and 314th) were committed to the air offensive against Japan, and on 14 May all four took part in a daylight attack on Nagoya. The same target was attacked again on 16/17 May, when 475 B-29s dropped 3,609 tons of incendiaries on the docks area. Each aircraft in the main force carried eight tons of M50 magnesium bombs. The destruction amounted to 3.8 square miles and included one of Mitsubishi's aircraft factories. It was the last time that devastated Nagoya was subjected to an aerial attack.

On 23 May, 21st Bomber Command launched its biggest attack so far. Late in the afternoon 562 Superfortresses took off from their bases in the Marianas, arriving over Tokyo shortly after midnight. Attacking through intense flak between 8,000 and 15,000 feet, they unloaded over 3,600 tons of napalm and oil bombs through nine-tenths cloud, smoke and the glare of searchlights, razing 5.3 square miles of the city. Four B-29s were shot down and sixty-nine damaged, all of them by anti-aircraft fire.

Two nights later Tokyo was subjected to its most fearful holocaust yet. A total of 502 aircraft dropped 3,262 tons of incendiaries on the enemy capital; vast firestorms raged through its shattered streets, destroying an area of 16.8 square miles. The Americans, however, did not have things all their own way. The flak was the heaviest ever

101

encountered by 21st Bomber Command, and the Japanese fighters were up in force; twenty-six B-29s failed to return and 100 more were damaged, many of them severely.

On 17/18 June, following a series of daylight precision attacks on targets in Japan's major cities, the weight of the strategic offensive was switched to Japan's smaller industrial towns. Between that night and the end of the war 21st Bomber Command flew 8,014 sorties against these targets, dropping 54,184 tons of incendiaries. Fifty-seven towns were attacked, thirty-five of them on nine nights in July, when the bombers destroyed a total area of 35.4 square miles.

The massive air attacks continued, even after the dropping of the two atomic bombs on Hiroshima and Nagasaki on 6 and 9 August. On 14 August 449 Superfortresses, escorted by 186 Mustangs and Thunderbolts, struck at the last remaining targets – the naval arsenal at Hikari, the Osaka Army Arsenal, the Marifu marshalling yards near Hiroshima and the Nippon Oil Co. plant at Atika. That night the B-29s carried out a heavy incendiary raid on Kumagaya and Isezaki, north-west of Tokyo.

Even before this raid took place the Japanese had decided to accept the Allies' unconditional surrender terms. The last hours were described by Japanese fighter ace Saburo Sakai, in his book *Samurai*.

'Japan was about to *surrender*.

'"Sakai." I looked up. "Saburo, it ... it is just about the end now." Kawachi spoke. "We have very little time left. Let us make one more flight together, one last flight." He kicked the ground idly with his foot. "We just can't quit like this," he protested. "We have to draw blood once more."

'I nodded. He was right. We told the maintenance men to move our two Zeros out to the runway, to prepare them for flight. We knew that the Superfortresses would bomb tonight. The weather forecast appeared promising, and there were so many bombers overhead every evening that B-29s could be intercepted almost anywhere. For a long time they had flown over Oppama without opposition, using the field for a landmark. They would not expect fighters.

'Kawachi and I kept our plans strictly to ourselves, not even telling the other pilots ... The afternoon passed and we remained seated, almost invisible in the darkness. Shortly after midnight the tower radio spluttered. "Alert. Alert. A B-29 formation is now approaching the Yokosuka-Tokyo area."

'We jumped to our feet and ran across the field to our planes. The air base lay in blackness, not a light showing. There was just enough light from the stars to enable us to make our way. When we reached the Zeros, we discovered that we were not the only pilots determined to go up for a

last mission. At least eight other fighters were lined up at the edge of the runway, fuelled and armed.

'The moment we were airborne, I swung in close to Kawachi's fighter and took up a position off his wing. Eight other Zeros were in the air with us, forming into two flights behind our planes. We climbed steadily, then circled at 10,000 feet over Tokyo Bay.

'Kawachi's fighter banked abruptly and pulled away to the east. I flew with him, the two flights close behind. For a few moments I failed to see any other planes in the air. Then Kawachi's cannon started firing, and I made out the big bomber flying northward. I had him now, clear in my sights. I pulled up almost alongside Kawachi's plane and opened fire. We each had four cannon now, and we would need every weapon against the tremendous airplane. I had never seen anything so huge! As I swung around after completing my firing pass, I saw the eight other fighters storming the Superfortress. They appeared like tiny gnats milling round a tremendous bull. How could we hope to shoot down an airplane of such incredible size?

'I came in again, climbing and sending my fire into the B-29's underside. The counterfire was terrible. Tracers spilled into the air from the multiple turrets of the B-29, and I felt the Zero shudder several times as the enemy gunners found their mark. We ignored the bomber's guns and kept pressing home the attack. The Superfortress turned and headed south. Apparently we had damaged the big plane, and now he was running for home. I clung to Kawachi and slammed the engine on overboost. The other eight fighters were already lost far behind us, and it was doubtful that we could keep up with the bomber. It possessed remarkable speed and was, in fact, faster than the Zero I had flown at Lae.

'Kawachi, however, had no intention of losing the big plane in the dark. He cut inside the B-29's wide turn and led me down in a shallow diving attack. This time we had a clear shot, and both Kawachi and I kept the triggers down, watching the tracers and shells ripping into the glass along the bomber's nose. We had him! Suddenly, the Superfortress's speed fell off and the pilot dropped the airplane down for a long dive. We came around in a tight turn, firing steadily in short bursts, pouring the cannon shells into the crippled plane.

'The great bomber descended quickly. I saw no fire or smoke. There was no visible damage, but the airplane continued to lose altitude steadily, dropping towards the ocean. We kept after the fleeing plane. O Shima island suddenly loomed up out of the darkness. We were fifty miles south of Yokosuka.

'We pulled up out of our dives, and climbed to 1,500 feet. A volcano on the island reared 1,000 feet above the water, and we dared not risk a collision in the blackness. I could make out the bomber faintly as it dropped. Presently it ditched with a splash of white foam in the ocean, several miles off O Shima's southern coastline. In less than a minute the B-29 disappeared beneath the water.

'Back at the airfield, we learned that at least three cities had been gutted during the night. The fires were still

Above and below: *The Yokosuka P1Y1 Ginga was a superb aircraft as a fast bomber, but an attempt to convert it into a night fighter proved disappointing.* (Philip Jarrett)

burning fiercely, unchecked, sweeping before the wind. 'The war was to end less than twelve hours later ...'

In summary, it is clear that the dwindling Japanese fighter force never had any real hope of halting the onslaught by the B-29 night bombers. But it might have inflicted considerably more damage on them, had it not been for a wrong decision made in the closing months of 1944.

The subject of the decision was the Yokosuka P1Y1 Ginga (Milky Way) fast twin-engined bomber. Known by the Allied code-name *Frances*, it was perhaps the nearest Japanese equivalent of the de Havilland Mosquito and the Ju 88. During its flight test programme, this aircraft, which had a top speed of 340 mph, attracted the attention of Japanese Navy pilots, who were attempting to create a night fighter force to counter expected bombing attacks. The Kawanishi company was instructed to produce a night fighter variant under the designation P1Y2-S; this was armed with a pair of 20 mm cannon, mounted obliquely in the upper fuselage, and retained the bomb bay of the Ginga for intruder operations. First flown in June 1944, the P1Y2-S went into production as the Navy Night Fighter Kyokko (Aurora), but its performance at altitude proved disappointing and the ninety-six examples built had their 20 mm cannon removed and reverted to the bomber role.

The Japanese had no means of knowing that most of the devastating B-29 attacks would be made from medium and low level, where the Kyokko might have shown its true potential.

CHAPTER TWELVE

POST-WAR DEVELOPMENTS, 1945–50

The United States

In the late summer of 1943, North American Aviation Inc began design work on an aircraft to meet a USAAF requirement for a twin-engined, long-range escort fighter for service in the Pacific Theatre. Part of the specification was that the aircraft should have two pilots to ease the strain of long over-water flights.

North American's simple solution was to join two P-51H Mustang fuselages by means of a new wing centre section, so creating a two-seat, twin-engined aircraft with greatly enhanced long-range performance. The USAAF liked the concept and ordered 500 examples of the production variant, designated P-82B, but with the sudden ending of the war this was cut back to just twenty examples for service

with the Air Defense Command. Eighteen were completed as P-82Bs, but the tenth and eleventh production aircraft were completed as P-82C and P-82D Twin Mustang night fighters for evaluation as replacements for the Northrop P-61 Black Widow in this role. The P-82C (44-65169) was fitted with an SCR720 AI radar in a large central pod, while the P-82D (44-65170) carried the APS-4. The radar operator sat in the right-hand cockpit at his AI console, the radar aerials being installed under the outer wing sections.

Trials with the two aircraft showed that the night fighter variant of the Twin Mustang would be more than adequate as a P-61 replacement, and in March 1946 orders were placed for an additional 250 aircraft. In the event, however, the first 100 were completed as escort and ground-attack

The North American F-82 Twin Mustang filled a crucial post-war night and all-weather fighter gap for the USAF. (Author)

The Bell XP-83 was proposed to meet a specification for a jet-propelled night fighter for the USAF, but it was outclassed by later designs. (Author)

fighters for the newly-established Strategic Air Command, which came into existence on 21 March 1946. Only ninety-one were completed as F-82F night fighters (the 'P' prefix now having been dropped by the USAF) with APS-4 radar, and fifty-nine as F-82Gs with the SCR-270. These aircraft, which were also fitted with APN-1 radar altimeters and APS-13 tail warning radars, equipped the 51st Fighter Interceptor Group (16th, 25th and 26th Squadrons), the 52nd All-Weather Fighter Group (2nd and 5th Squadrons), the 325th All-Weather Fighter Group (317th, 318th and 319th Squadrons), and the 84th Reserve Fighter Group (496th, 497th and 498th Squadrons).

In the Far East, Twin Mustangs were also assigned to the 4th Fighter Squadron (All-Weather) at Naha on Okinawa, the 68th Fighter Squadron (All-Weather) at Itazuke on Kyushu, and the 339th Fighter Squadron (All-Weather) at Yokota, near Tokyo. As we shall see in the next chapter, the Twin Mustangs were to play a vital part in the early, critical phase of the Korean War.

The Twin Mustang, however, was in reality an interim aircraft, pending the development of a suitable jet-propelled night fighter. The USAF issued a specification for such an aircraft in May 1946; among possible early candidates was the Bell XP-83, which began life as a heavy single-seat long-range fighter and flew for the first time on 25

February 1945, powered by two General Electric J33-GE-5 turbojets. Two prototypes were built and extensively tested, their performance figures including a maximum speed of 525 mph at 45,000 feet, together with a range of 1,730 miles at 30,000 feet. The proposed armament for the XP-83 was six 0.5 in machine-guns, with either four 20 mm or four 37 mm cannon as alternatives. The XP-83's airframe had the potential for conversion to a two-seat configuration and the inclusion of AI radar, but there would have been a substantial weight penalty and the existing engines were not powerful enough. This, together with the fact that the XP-83 was outclassed by later designs, led to development being abandoned.

Meanwhile, three American aircraft companies, Curtiss, Northrop and Lockheed, were busy working up designs to meet the USAF requirement, which called for a two-seat radar-equipped aircraft armed with either cannon or machine-guns and possessing a top speed of at least 600 mph and a ceiling of 40,000 feet.

The design submitted by the Airplane Division of the Curtiss-Wright Corporation, the XP-87, was the first multi-seat jet combat aircraft specifically designed for the radar intercept role at night. Developed from an earlier wartime project, the XA-43 attack aircraft, it was powered by four Westinghouse XJ34-WE-7 turbojets, installed in

This page and following page: *The Northrop F-89 Scorpion was the mainstay of USAF Air Defense Command during most of the 1950s.* (Philip Jarrett)

pairs in two nacelles, and was armed with four 20 mm cannon. Provision was also made to install 0.5 in machine guns in a dorsal turret, but this was never fitted. The XP-87 prototype (49-59600) flew for the first time on 5 March 1948, and work began on a second aircraft, the XP-87A, which was intended to have two General Electric J47-GE-15 engines. The first aircraft was known as the Nighthawk, the second as the Blackhawk. However, the second machine never flew, and an order for eighty-eight J47-powered production aircraft was cancelled to release funds for the development of two more promising designs that were eventually to give the USAF a truly potent night/all-weather capability, the Lockheed F-94C Starfire and the Northrop F-89 Scorpion. The XP-87 passed into aviation history as the last combat aircraft produced by Curtiss-Wright.

The first of two Northrop XF-89 prototypes flew on 16 August 1948, and after USAF evaluation Northrop received an order for an initial batch of forty-eight production aircraft. The first of these flew late in 1950 and deliveries to the United States Air Force Air Defense Command began soon afterwards, the first Scorpion squadrons being assigned to Arctic defence zones such as Alaska, Iceland and Greenland. The first production model of the Scorpion, the F-89A, was powered by two Allison J35-A-21 turbojets with reheat and carried a nose armament of six 20 mm cannon. The F-89B and F-89C were progressive developments with uprated

Allison engines, while the F-89D had its cannon deleted and carried an armament of 104 folding-fin aircraft rockets (FFAR) in wingtip pods. Additional fuel tanks under the wings gave an eleven per cent range increase over the F-89C and the aircraft was fitted with an automatic fire control system. The F-89H, which followed the F-89D into production, was armed with six Hughes GAR-1 Falcon missiles and forty-two FFAR, and could also carry the MB-1 Genie nuclear AAM. The Falcons were housed in the wingtip pods and were extended prior to firing. The F-89H's armament was fired automatically, a sighting radar and fire control computer forming a fully integrated attack system.

The other night/all-weather design conceived in the 1940s, the Lockheed F-94 Starfire, was developed from the T-33A trainer, two production T-33 airframes being converted as YF-94s. The first of these flew on 16 April 1949, and four months later the USAF placed contracts for seventeen F-94A-1-LO and ninety-two F-94A-5-LO fighters, together with one YF-94B – the latter having centrally-mounted wingtip tanks instead of underslung tanks.

The F-94A, which incorporated seventy-five per cent of the components used in the T-33 and F-80 Shooting Star, had 940 lb of radar equipment in the nose and an armament of four 0.50 in Colt-Browning machine-guns. The aircraft was powered by an Allison J33-A-33 centrifugal-type turbojet with reheat. F-94As were fitted with 195 imp gal Fletcher wingtip tanks. The F-94A went into

The Lockheed F-94 Starfire, with its powerful missile armament, brought a new dimension to the USAF's night and all-weather capability.
(Philip Jarrett)

production in 1949; 200 were built, the first entering service in June 1950 with the 319th All-
Weather Fighter Squadron.

The YF-94B was converted from the nineteenth
F-94A in 1950, and 357 F-94Bs were built. Apart
from the revised wingtip tanks, they differed from
the F-94A mainly in having a modified hydraulics
system and avionics, including a Sperry Zero-
Reader flight recorder. The next variant, the
F-94C, differed so extensively from its predecessors
that it was originally known as the YF-97A. This
designation remained in force from the aircraft's
maiden flight on 16 January 1950 until 12
September that year, when the designation YF-94C
was officially adopted.

The F-94C was fitted with an afterburning Pratt
& Whitney J48-P-5, and other changes included an
increase in wing dihedral and a reduction in thick-
ness/chord ratio from thirteen to ten per cent, the
introduction of a swept tailplane, and the replacement of the gun armament by twenty-four
unguided FFAR in a ring of tubes around the nose-
cone. Later, provision was made for a further
twenty-four rockets in wing pods. The F-94C
carried 1,200 lb of electronics, and two 1,000 lb

*The 'black boxes' that brought the F-94 to its target; the system had
as many different parts as 200 TV sets.* (Philip Jarrett)

F-94C Starfires being made ready for delivery to the US Air Defense Command. (Philip Jarrett)

thrust RATOG (rocket assisted take-off gear) packs could be fitted under the fuselage. Total production of the F-94C came to 387 aircraft before the series was completed in 1954.

Great Britain

In January 1946 six squadrons – Nos 23, 25, 29, 85, 141 and 264 – were responsible for the night defence of Britain. All of them were armed, or in the process of rearming, with the de Havilland Mosquito NF36. With the advent of jet aircraft, it was apparent that the Mosquito needed to be urgently replaced, and in December 1946 the Air Staff issued Operational Requirement OR227, calling for a jet-propelled, twin-engined, two-seat night and all-weather fighter. (Another requirement, OR228, covered a replacement for the Gloster Meteor in the day fighter role; it would eventually be met by the Hawker Hunter).

In January 1947 OR227 crystallised into Specification F44/66, modified to F4/48 a year or

so later, but none of the early proposals submitted satisfied the requirement, so the Gloster Aircraft Company was asked to investigate the possibility of developing a night/all-weather version of the Meteor to bridge the gap. Gloster had already carried out radar installation trials on Meteor F3 and F4 aircraft in conjunction with the Telecommunications Research Establishment, and the Company now looked to the two-seat Meteor T7 airframe as a suitable vehicle for adaptation to night fighter configuration.

Specification F24/48 was issued and written around the Gloster aircraft, and the fourth production Meteor T7 was converted as an aerodynamic prototype, flying in October 1949. The first true prototype of the Meteor NF11, as the night fighter variant was designated, flew on 31 May 1950. The aircraft featured the T7's tandem cockpit, the F8's tail unit and long-span wings similar to those of the PR10 high-altitude photo-reconnaissance version, and was fitted with a lengthened di-electric nose containing the scanner for the AI Mk X radar. This equipment, of American origin (it was the SCR720

The Meteor NF11 prototype was based on the T7 trainer airframe, with the addition of a Mk 8 tail unit. (Philip Jarrett)

This plan view of the Meteor NF11 clearly shows the 20 mm cannon mounted in the outer wing panels. (Philip Jarrett)

The de Havilland Sea Hornet NF Mk 21 prototype, PX230. The aircraft was used by No 809 Squadron until 1954, when it was replaced by the Sea Venom. (Philip Jarrett)

The Vampire NF10 was initiated as a private venture by de Havilland. The prototype and demonstrator aircraft is seen here. (Philip Jarrett)

set carried by the Black Widow) was the same as that fitted in the Mosquito NF36; it had proved very effective in the closing stages of World War II, but by 1950 its performance was rapidly degrading. Its use was dictated by the failure of the British Mk IXc, developed by TRE at Malvern; far better AI equipment was being produced by the American company, Westinghouse, but although it would be ordered later for use in later marks of Meteor no attempt to purchase it was made at this stage.

As Gloster was fully occupied in building the Meteor F8 day fighter, and in working on the prototype of the aircraft that would eventually meet F4/48 – the GA5, later to be called the Javelin – it was decided to transfer responsibility for NF11 production to Armstrong Whitworth. The first production Meteor NF11 (WD585) was delivered to No 29 Squadron at Tangmere in August 1951; the operational career of the NF11 and the follow-on Meteor night fighter marks will be examined in chapter fourteen.

De Havilland produced two night fighter types in the late 1940s. The first was the Sea Hornet NF21, developed in 1946 to meet an urgent need for a high-performance night fighter for the Royal Navy. After lengthy trials this variant entered service with No 809 Squadron at Culdrose in January 1949, the unit embarking on HMS *Vengeance* in May 1951. The Sea Hornet NF21 was used by 809 Squadron until 1954, when it was replaced by the Sea Venom.

The other de Havilland night fighter type was the Vampire NF10, which served with both the RAF and the Italian Air Force. The NF10 entered service with Nos 23, 25 and 151 Squadrons, which

used it for a short period before it was replaced by other types.

The Soviet Union

During World War II, the Soviet Air Force had no aircraft designed specifically for night fighting. During the aerial battles that took place over Moscow and Leningrad in 1941, and later over Stalingrad, some converted Pe-2 dive bombers were used in the night fighter role, as was a heavily-armed interceptor variant, the Pe-3, but the Russians had no AI equipment and had to depend on visual interception techniques.

It was not until 1948 that the Russians, with the help of German technology, succeeded in developing a viable AI radar known as *Izumrud* (Emerald), which was intended to equip a new generation of night and all-weather fighter aircraft. Pavel Sukhoi, whose Su-9 twin-jet fighter prototype had flown in 1946, now came up with the Su-15, also known as the *Samolyot* (aircraft) P. Powered by two RD-45 (Rolls-Royce Nene) turbojets, the aircraft had a mid-mounted wing with a leading-edge sweep of thirty-seven degrees, the twin engines being mounted one above the other in a deep centre fuselage, and exhausting below the fuselage aft of the wing trailing edge. The AI scanner was housed in a small radome situated above the nose air intake, and armament was two 37 mm cannon, one mounted on either side of the nose. With a loaded weight of 23,000 lb the Su-15 was a very heavy aircraft; nevertheless, its designers estimated that it would have a maximum speed of 641 mph, a service

The twin-engined Suckhoi Su-15, also known as the Samolyot-P, was fitted with Izumrud (Emerald) *AI radar. The sole prototype was destroyed during flight testing.* (Author)

Mikoyan's I-320(R) all-weather fighter was based on the MiG-15. Its flight characteristics were poor and it was abandoned. (via Author)

ceiling of 46,000 feet, and the ability to reach 32,800 feet in six and a half minutes.

These figures were never proven, because the Su-15 disintegrated following severe vibration on an early high-speed run, the pilot ejecting, and no further prototypes were built.

The other main contenders in the race to produce a Russian night fighter were Mikoyan, Lavochkin and and Yakovlev. Mikoyan's design, the single-seat I-320(R), was powered by two Klimov VK-1 turbojets and first flew in 1949; it was based on the MiG-15, but the engine installation resulted in a bulky, ungainly aircraft with poor handling characteristics and even worse visibility for the pilot, whose forward view was badly obscured by the long nose and radome. Lavochkin's design, the La-200A, was a better proposition from several points of view, but suffered from the same engine arrangement as the I-320(R). In both cases, the VK-1 engines were fed via a common nose air intake, but in the La-200A they were installed in tandem, the first exhausting under the fuselage and the second under the tail, and this necessitated some complex ducting that resulted in an inordinately large fuselage. A central air intake cone housed the La-200A's *Izumrud* radar and the fighter

The La-200B was designed to the same requirement as the Yak-25, to which it proved inferior. With its massive radome, it was one of the ugliest fighter aircraft ever built. (via Author)

was a two-seater, the pilot and radar observer seated side by side. The La-200A had a fuselage-mounted undercarriage and carried an armament of three 37 mm cannon, which contributed to the high all-up weight of 22,873 lb. Like the I-320(R), the La-200A flew in 1949, and during trials reached a maximum speed of 660 mph at 16,400 feet; the service ceiling was 59,700 feet. Neither aircraft underwent extensive operational trials, because in 1950 a developed, lighter version of the *Izumrud* AI radar was successfully installed in a two-seat MiG-15 variant known as the SP-5; both MiG-15s and MiG-17s were subsequently equipped with AI.

These variants, however, did not meet the urgent requirement for an all-weather fighter fitted with long-range AI radar, and a specification for such an aircraft was issued in November 1951. Lavochkin set about modifying the La-200A to carry a new radar scanner in a lengthened fuselage nose, and the result was the La-200B, one of the ugliest fighter aircraft ever flown. The massive radome ruled out a single air intake, so the engines were fed by three ducts, one on either side of the nose and one underneath it. Bulky auxiliary fuel tanks were fitted under the wings, and to compensate for the extra weight – the aircraft now weighed 24,750 lb loaded – the undercarriage was strengthened.

The La-200B was not the solution to the Soviet Air Force's night and all-weather interception problems. That still lay over the horizon, and it would be provided by Alexander S. Yakovlev – the designer who, above all others, had given the Russians fighter superiority over the Eastern Front.

CHAPTER THIRTEEN

NIGHT BATTLE OVER KOREA

When Communist North Korean forces launched their surprise attack on the Republic of Korea (ROK) on 25 June 1950, one of the first priorities was to evacuate US and other foreign nationals from the South Korean capital, Seoul. A number of freighters were already standing by in Inchon harbour, ready to take the evacuees to safety in Japan, and in the early hours of 26 June, with North Korean tanks only a few miles from Seoul, General Douglas MacArthur, the Supreme Commander Allied Powers in the Pacific Theatre, ordered General Earle T. Partridge, the United States Fifth Air Force Commander, to provide air cover over the evacuation area.

The only aircraft really suitable for the patrol task, because of the distances involved from the Japanese airfields, were the long-range F-82s of the 68th Fighter All-Weather Squadron at Itazuke on Kyushu, but there were only twelve of them, too few to carry out effective standing patrols. In an effort to resolve the problem, General Partridge ordered the 339th All-Weather Squadron to redeploy its F-82s from Yokota to Itazuke, and also requested the Twentieth Air Force to despatch eight F-82s of the 4th Squadron to Itazuke from their base on Okinawa.

The evacuation got under way at first light on 26 June, the majority of the refugees embarking on a Norwegian vessel. Overhead, the F-82s circled watchfully in flights of four, a few hundred feet below the cloud base. The evacuation proceeded without interference during the morning, but at 13.30 there was a sudden alarm when a North Korean La-7 fighter dropped down out of the clouds and attacked a flight of F-82s. The American fighter pilots took evasive action, and after this single pass the enemy fighter climbed steeply back into the clouds and disappeared. This action was taken to present a direct threat to the evacuation, and during the remainder of the day the F-82s ventured inland to cover evacuation convoys *en route* from Seoul to Inchon. After dark the fighters

Crews of the 339th FS (all-weather) in the process of converting from Northrop P-61 Black Widows to North American F-82 Twin Mustangs at Johnson AB, Japan, in 1949, some months before the outbreak of the Korean War. (Martin Bambrick)

North American F-82G Twin Mustang on patrol over Korea, 1950. (Robert F. Dorr)

continued to accompany the merchantman as it headed out into the Yellow Sea, only breaking contact when the ship was met by an escort of American destroyers. On the 27th, the maritime patrol task off the Korean coast was assumed by Navy Patrol Squadron VP-47, based at Iwakuni and equipped with Martin PBM-5 Mariners.

The airlift of evacuees from Seoul and Kimpo also got under way on 27 June, the day on which United States President Harry Truman ordered sea and air forces in the Far East to give support and cover to the ROK forces, in effect authorising an armed conflict if necessary. Finding transport aircraft to carry out the airlift had presented something of a problem; the C-54s of the 374th Wing were widely dispersed on routine duties, and only two were immediately available. The situation was saved by the arrival of eleven C-47s, hastily assembled from various FEAF (Far East Air Force) transport units. The first transports took off from Itazuke before dawn, escorted by F-82s. At daybreak, while the transports landed at Kimpo and Suwon under the protection of the Twin Mustangs, two flights of F-80 Shooting Stars of the 8th Fighter Bomber Wing arrived over the Han river and began a high-level patrol, covering the approaches to the South Korean capital.

The patrolling fighters encountered no enemy opposition until midday, when five Yak-7s appeared over Seoul and initiated an attack on Kimpo. They were intercepted by five F-82s of the 68th and 339th Squadrons, and in a five-minute air battle

three Yaks were shot down, the first by Lieutenant William G. Hudson of the 68th Squadron, to whom fell the distinction of destroying the first communist aircraft over Korea. The other American pilots who scored were Major James W. Little and Lieutenant Charles B. Moran.

The Twin Mustang featured prominently in the 'shopping list' of reinforcement aircraft sent to Washington at the end of June 1950, but the USAF was unable to meet the requirement for additional aircraft. There were only 168 F-82s in service, and apart from the fact that most were needed for the all-weather defence of the continental United States (a role they would continue to fulfil until the deployment of the Northrop F-89 Scorpion from 1950) there was a critical shortage of spares, which frustrated any move to make good the attrition suffered by the Fifth AF's F-82s in Korea.

During the bitter winter of 1950–51, a winter that saw the massive involvement of Chinese troops in Korea, night intruder operations were carried out by Douglas B-26 Invaders of the 3rd Bombardment Wing, while the night air defence task was assumed by two squadrons of the Marine Air Wing. One of these, VMF(N)-513, was armed with F4U-5N Corsairs; the other, VMF(N)-542, with F7F-3N Tigercats. In March 1951 VMF(N)-542 returned to El Toro, California, to rearm with the Douglas F3D-1 Skyknight jet night fighter; its Tigercats were assigned to VMF(N)-513, together with a pair of F-82 Twin Mustangs. The unit retained its Corsairs, which operated by day in the

Douglas B-26 Invaders of the 3rd Bombardment Wing carried out night intruder operations. (Robert F. Dorr)

The Grumman F7F Tigercat night fighter served with VMF(N)-542 and -513 in Korea. (Author)

ground-attack role.

During World War II, the Russians had made extensive use of light aircraft, notably Polikarpov Po-2 biplanes, to carry out night attacks on German positions and installations on the Eastern Front. Within a year of the outbreak of hostilities in Korea, once the front line had stabilised, the North Korean Air Force adopted similar tactics.

The first of these nuisance raids took place in the early hours of 14 June 1951, when two Polikarpov Po-2s took off from Sariwon airstrip. One attacked Suwon, dropping two bombs that narrowly missed the runway, and the other released its bombs on an Eighth Army motor transport park at Inchon, causing splinter damage to several vehicles. On the next night a third raider – identified as an MBR-2 amphibian – made a low-level strafing run over Kimpo airfield, fortunately without hitting anything.

The next attack, on 16/17 June, produced spectacular results. On this occasion, two Po-2s led by Lieutenant La Woon Yung arrived over Suwon, the crews finding to their surprise that the airfield was brightly lit. La Woon Yung had no difficulty in picking out the F-86 Sabres of the 4th Fighter Interceptor Wing in their dispersals and dropped his pair of bombs on a flight of 335th Squadron aircraft, destroying one Sabre and damaging eight others, four of them seriously. The other pilot dropped his bombs on the parked vehicles of the 802nd Engineer Aviation Battalion, severely damaging several of them.

The nightly visits by the Po-2 raiders, nicknamed 'Bed Check Charlies', continued to be a thorn in the Allies' flesh throughout the summer of 1951, and steps were taken to combat them. The biplanes, cruising at 80 knots and at low level down the valleys on the approach to their targets, proved incredibly difficult to detect by radar, and when night fighters were sent up to intercept them the Po-2 pilots made full use of their low speed and high manoeuvrability to evade them. However, two

F4U-5N Corsair night fighters of Composite Squadron VC-3 on a carrier in Yokosuka Bay, Japan, during the Korean War (Robert F. Dorr)

Po-2s were intercepted and destroyed during June 1951; the first on the night of the 23rd by Captain Dick Heyman, flying a B-26 of the 8th Squadron, and the second on the 30th over the Han river by Captain E.B. Long of Marine Squadron VMF(N)-513, flying an F7F Tigercat. His radar intercept officer (RIO), Warrant Officer R.C. Buckingham, steered him to the black-painted target, which he shot down on his third pass after reducing speed to the absolute safe minimum. It was the Tigercat's first combat victory.

Shortly after midnight on 12 July, a Corsair night fighter of VMF(N)-513 surprised a Po-2 raider and shot it down in flames over Seoul. This success was followed, on 23 September, by another scored by an F7F Tigercat. A Po-2 had attacked Kimpo in the early hours and was intercepted by Major Eugene A. Van Gundy and his RIO, Master Sergeant T.H. Ullom. Van Gundy closed in to 500 feet and destroyed the enemy aircraft with 20 mm cannon fire.

Fears of large-scale enemy air attacks on Allied air bases in Korea proved unfounded, but the nuisance raids by Po-2s continued to keep the night defences on the alert. Four T-6 Texans armed with .30 calibre machine-guns were kept on readiness at Kimpo during the hours of darkness, but they never had any luck; neither did the 68th Fighter Interceptor Squadron's (FIS) Lockheed F-94B Starfires, which replaced the unit's North American F-82 Twin Mustangs in December 1951. Two F-94s were deployed to Suwon, where they were joined in March 1952 by the 319th FIS, whose F-94s were deployed to Korea from McChord AFB, Tacoma, Washington. One F-94 did manage to shoot down a Po-2 by throttling right back and lowering landing gear and flaps to reduce its speed, but it stalled immediately afterwards and spun into the ground, killing its crew. Another F-94 was lost when it collided with a Po-2.

Royal Navy Fairey Fireflies also joined the battle against the night intruders towards the end of the war in Korea. An observer with No 810 Squadron, R.K. Simmons, on HMS *Ocean* recalls that:

'On 7 July 1953 I was detached with the CO, Lieutenant Cdr A.W. Bloomer, RN, to the 319th FIS at K-13 (Suwon) to determine whether the Firefly V could be used as an interceptor to counter the threat posed by Po-2s which were operating from road strips just short of the front line. These aircraft were flying at night just below the level of the air defence radar, with ladies in the back throwing out 40 lb bombs by hand. We were patrolling at night with wheels and flaps down at 95 knots, just above the stall.

Boeing B-29s of FEAF Bomber Command on a daylight mission to North Korea. Communist MiG-15 night fighters came near to sweeping the B-29s from Korea's night skies. (Robert F. Dorr)

'It was soon found impracticable to operate the Firefly from a jet base, so we were transferred to K-6 (Pyongtaek-ni) with Marine Air Group 12. We had no luck with Po-2s; indeed, the only bogey we had managed to outpace us, and was believed to be a Yak-9.

'It is interesting to note that the 319th FIS was supposed to have a complement of twenty-four aircraft. In fact they were reduced to eighteen aircraft after a number of landing accidents. During the time I was with them they managed a maximum serviceability rate of six aircraft, and frequently could put only two aircraft into the sky. The squadron had a complement of 117 aircrew (i.e. about fifty-eight crews) who were lucky to get a flight once every ten days. With so little flying practice it was no wonder that many aircraft were damaged in landing accidents when weather was marginal.'

Late on in the war the Po-2s were joined by other training types, notably Yak-18s. Their heckling missions reached a climax of success on 16/17 June 1953, when they destroyed five million gallons of fuel in a dump at Inchon. Between 30 June and 16 July Lieutenant Guy P. Bordelon, a pilot with an F4U-5N detachment of VC-3 deployed to K-6 from the USS *Princeton* for anti-intruder operations, destroyed three Yak-18s and two other aircraft (either Lavochkin La-9s or La-11s) in the Seoul area. He was the USN's only ace of the Korean War.

Almost from the beginning of hostilities in Korea, targets in enemy territory were attacked by B-29 Superfortresses of the United States Far East

Air Force Bomber Command, assisted by Strategic Air Command (SAC) units deployed from the United States. Despite the fact that these attacks were carried out in daylight, often against strong opposition from MiG-15 fighters and flak, the Command lost only six B-29s in action between the beginning of the conflict and October 1951, but when that month ended five more had been destroyed by flak or fighters and eight others seriously damaged. In one week, fifty-five aircrew had been posted dead or missing and twelve others had been wounded. The aircrew losses were particularly serious, because by now the B-29 units in the Korean theatre were having to rely heavily on Air Force Reserve personnel who had flown B-29s during World War II in order to avoid an unacceptable drain on SAC's aircrew resources.

The outcome was inevitable; the B-29 force was restricted to night operations. By the end of November 1951 most of the Superfortresses had been fitted with Shoran short-range air navigation and bombing equipment, and although early Shoran night raids met with only limited success, the B-29s soon began to inflict heavy damage on the North Korean airfields. The enemy set up heavy flak batteries along the arcs followed by the bombers on their radar bombing runs, but although several B-29s were damaged none was lost. As yet, the communists possessed no effective night fighter force; the few night interceptions reported by the B-29 crews were carried out on a hit-or-miss basis by MiG-15s, relying on searchlights to

Top and above: *B-29s of Far East Air Forces Bomber Command attacking targets in North Korea.* (Author)

illuminate their targets. The only B-29 lost in November was on a leaflet dropping mission along the Yalu; it was hit by flak but succeeded in reaching the coast, where its crew parachuted to safety.

During these latter weeks it was clear that the communists were making extensive use of radar in carrying out their fighter interceptions. On several occasions, Allied fighter bombers were attacked by MiGs which dropped down through a cloud layer, obviously vectored to their targets by radar controllers. Early warning radars had been in place since December 1950, and had been identified by 91st Strategic Reconnaissance Wing RB-29 reconnaissance aircraft as being American-manufactured SCR-270 sets, supplied to the Soviet Union under lend-lease during World War II. They had an effective range of about 150 miles, but were able to detect an aircraft flying higher than 40,000 feet at a greater range. Another American-built radar, the SCR-584, formed a second component of the system, automatically tracking an intruding aircraft detected by the SCR-270 and directing anti-aircraft fire on to it.

The ground controlled interception (GCI) radar identified in 1952, however, was of Russian design and was code-named *Token*, and it was better than anything that had been deployed previously. The communists lost no time in using it to develop countermeasures against the B-29 night strikes; hitherto, such countermeasures had taken the form of searchlight and anti-aircraft batteries directed by the SCR-584 stations, but by the end of May 1952 the deployment of *Token* made it possible for the enemy to form at least one specialist night fighter unit, using Tupolev Tu-2 light bombers equipped with AI radar. These aircraft assumed the role of master night fighters; having located the bomber stream they would fly immediately above it and control the final interception phase, the other fighters having been guided to the scene by *Token*. The B-29s would then be constantly tracked by searchlight batteries, with the aid of which the night fighters would launch their attacks.

These tactics produced results. On 10 June 1952, four B-29s of the 19th BW were suddenly illuminated by twenty-four searchlights after being shadowed for some minutes by an unidentified aircraft. A few moments later they were attacked by twelve MiG-15s. One B-29 exploded over the target, a railway bridge at Kwaksan, and another went down somewhere over North Korea. A third was so badly damaged that it barely made an emergency landing at Kimpo. The fourth aircraft used countermeasures to break the searchlights' radar lock and got away unharmed.

Because of the growing danger from enemy defences, FEAF Bomber Command's operations were now restricted to nights when there was substantial cloud cover in the target areas. This was predicted when thirty B-29s set out to bomb the power plant at Suiho on 12/13 September 1952, but when the bombers reached the objective they found the skies clear. Six more B-29s orbited to the east of Suiho, jamming the enemy radars with electronic countermeasures, but the enemy put up a very concentrated box barrage and several of the attacking bombers were damaged. A few bombers were illuminated by searchlights, and one 307th Wing aircraft was shot down by night fighters. The other B-29s destroyed the target with 2,000 lb bombs.

A further threat to Bomber Command's night operations over north-west Korea developed in December 1952, when FEAF Intelligence received strong indications that two Russian night fighter squadrons had been deployed to the Antung airfield complex and were already in operation. Between 18 November 1952 and 31 January 1953 the communist air defences achieved notable successes at night, destroying five B-29s and damaging three more so badly that they had to be withdrawn from service. In the words of the official history:

'On the night of 18/19 November 1952 the Reds revealed new tactics when they shot down a 98th Wing B-29 coming off its supply-centre target at Sonchon. Riding above the B-29, a Red spotter dropped flares every time the bomber changed direction. The flares allowed searchlights to lock on the bomber, and four Red fighter passes riddled the bomber, forcing its crew to abandon ship over Cho-do. On the night of 30/31 December, when a full moon was at its zenith and contrails were streaming at bombing altitudes, Red searchlights coned three 19th Group B-29s which were attacking an ore-processing plant near the Yalu at Choak-tong. A conventional airplane called signals from above the bombers, and Red fighters shot down one B-29 and damaged two others so badly that their crews were forced down at Suwon. Bomber Command blamed the moonlight and the contrails for the losses, but in the dark of the moon on the night of 10/11 January 1953 a 307th Wing B-29 was coned by searchlights, hit by flak, and shot down by fighters over Anju's marshalling yards. The position of this bomber was apparently betrayed by light contrails.

'On the night of 12 January Red fighters intercepted and shot down a lone 91st Reconnaissance Squadron RB-29 which was distributing leaflets along the Yalu. On 28/29 January enemy fighters apparently silhouetted a 19th Group B-29 against a full moon over Kimpodong and needed no other illumination to shoot it down. Moonlight again betrayed 307th Wing B-29s when they bombed the Unjong-ni supply area on the night of 30/31 January. Some ten Red fighters prosecuted attacks which so badly damaged a B-29 that it barely made an emergency landing in South Korea. The total number of Red interceptions was not great. Bomber Command reported only twenty non-firing and twenty-three firing passes made

The Douglas F3D Skynight flew effective bomber support night missions over Korea from November 1952. (Author)

against its aircraft in January 1953. But the Red night interceptions were becoming extremely effective.

'Darkness was no longer affording the old B-29s the protection they needed to attack targets in North Korea ...'

Nevertheless, Bomber Command was to lose no more B-29s to enemy action after January 1953. This was due to a number of countermeasures as well as to natural causes, such as the raising of the contrail-forming level with the onset of spring. Attacks were arranged on an irregular basis; attack altitudes were varied as much as Shoran direction allowed; the bomber stream was compressed so that attacking aircraft passed through the target area in the minimum time; contrail-forming altitudes were avoided, and heavily defended targets were attacked as far as possible in the dark of the moon.

Another solution to the enemy night fighter problem was to provide bomber support, using night intruders to penetrate deep into enemy territory. Since June 1952 Marine Fighter Squadron VMF(N)-513 had been making four F7F Tigercats available for bomber support each night,

the fighters preceding the bomber stream by about five minutes in the run-up to the target area. They proved ineffective against the enemy's MiG-15s, and it was not until VMF(N)-513 re-equipped with twelve Douglas F3D-2N Skynights early in November 1952 that matters began to improve.

On 3/4 November, during the Skynight's second bomber support mission, Major William T. Stratton Jr, was brought to within visual range of a target by his radar operator, Master Sergeant Hans Hoglind. Stratton put three bursts of cannon fire into it and it went down in flames. The enemy aircraft was identified as a Yak-15 (Russia's first jet fighter), which is unlikely; it was more probably a piston-engined Yak-9 or a Yak-3, from which the Yak-15 was developed. Five nights later another Skynight crew destroyed an enemy aircraft, believed to have been a MiG-15, near Sonchon.

Later in November, General Hoyt S. Vandenberg, the USAF Chief of Staff, personally authorised the removal of the restrictions that had hitherto prevented the 319th Fighter Interceptor Squadron's F-94 Starfires from operating over enemy territory for fear that their modern fire

123

A Lockheed F-94 Starfire of the 319th FIS. Its crew, Capt Ben Fithian and Lt Sam Lyons (RO) were credited with the first Starfire kill over Korea. (Author)

control system might fall into enemy hands. From then on, flights of four to six F-94s flew barrier patrols about thirty miles ahead of the bomber stream while the Skynights took up position 2,000 to 3,000 feet above the bombers. These new tactics quickly produced results, the Skynights scoring two kills in moonlight conditions, one each on the nights of 28 and 31 January 1953. On the night of 30 January Captain Ben Fithian and Lieutenant Sam R. Lyons scored the F-94's first kill in Korea, shooting down an La-9. Between them, the Skynights and Starfires destroyed fifteen enemy aircraft in the first half of 1953. It was a relatively small contribution in terms of enemy aircraft destroyed, but it helped the war-weary B-29s to survive those last months of conflict in Korea.

Another factor that helped the B-29s to survive was electronic countermeasures, the development of which was accelerated by FEAF after June 1952.

Data on enemy radars and electronic systems, collected by the 'ferret' RB-29s of the 91st SRS, was collated, evaluated and disseminated by a special section of the 548th Reconnaissance Technical Squadron. Despite the use of old equipment and partly-trained operators, Bomber Command's ECM programme produced results. Between 1 January and 27 July 1953, in the course of 534 B-29 sorties, 114 aircraft were illuminated by searchlights, and in at least eighty-seven cases the searchlight lock was broken by the use of ECM. Had ECM not been available, Bomber Command's losses would almost certainly have been triple what they were. And there was another inescapable fact. If the communists had possessed an effective night/all-weather air defence system – or even if they had used the existing one properly – the night sky over North Korea might have been completely denied to United Nations bombers.

CHAPTER FOURTEEN

COLD WAR

The Yakovlev Yak-25 Flashlight *was the mainstay of the Soviet Air Force's night/all-weather interceptor force during the 1950s.*
(Philip Jarrett)

The failure of the communist air defences to stem the B-29 night offensive against targets in North Korea did not pass unnoticed in the Soviet Union. Neither did the fact that American reconnaissance aircraft like the RB-29, RB-36 and RB-50 were making frequent night incursions into Soviet airspace, radar-mapping Russian airfields and other facilities. These two facts combined to accelerate the development of a viable Soviet night and all-weather jet fighter, and there were only two real contenders. The first, as we have seen, was the unwieldy Lavochkin La-200B; the second was the Yakovlev Yak-25, and it was this aircraft that was selected for production, although not without a good deal of political lobbying by the Yakovlev design team. The problem was that Semyon Lavochkin had the backing of Lavrenti Beria, the all-powerful Soviet Chief of Secret Police; but Yakovlev went directly to Josef Stalin, and managed to win him over.

In every respect, the Yak-25 was a better aircraft than the La-200B. A mid-wing monoplane with forty-five degrees of sweep, it was a tandem two-seater and featured a bicycle undercarriage with outriggers under the wings. It was fitted with an improved version of the *Izumrud* AI radar under a large plastic radome and was armed with two 30 mm cannon mounted under the fuselage. The Yak-25 prototypes had two 6,000 lb static thrust (s.t.) Mikulin AM-5 engines, but production aircraft had the more powerful AM-5F, the F denoting *Forsazh*, or reheat. Several prototypes were flying by the summer of 1952 and the aircraft entered service with a Soviet Air Force development unit in 1955, becoming fully operational in the following year. The Yak-25 was allotted the NATO code-name *Flashlight*.

The Yak-25 was to be the mainstay of the Soviet Air Force's night/all-weather fighter force throughout the 1950s, and in that role it was complemented by the shorter-range MiG-19 Farmer, a night fighter variant of Russia's first truly supersonic jet-fighter having been produced. By the late 1950s, however, an extra requirement had been built into specifications for a new generation of Soviet night and all-weather fighters: extended combat radius. No longer was it necessary for American strategic bombers to penetrate into Soviet airspace; they were now armed with stand-off missiles that could be launched from points well outside Soviet territory, and the priority of the IA-PVO, the Soviet Air Force's Air Defence Command, was to destroy SAC's B-52 bombers before they came within launch range.

Soviet Intelligence circles were doubtless well aware, at an early stage, that the USAF was developing such weapons. In the mid-1950s, the Bell Aircraft Corporation had extensively tested an air-launched strategic missile, the XB-63 Rascal, which was designed to be carried by a modified version of the B-47 Stratojet known as the DB-47. The missile, which was capable of 1.6 M and had a stand-off range of about seventy-five miles, made some forty test flights from DB-36 and DB-47 carrier aircraft between 1953 and 1957, and by the end of the series was achieving a 1,500-foot circular error probable (CEP), which was acceptable with a nuclear warhead. SAC's entire Rascal programme was to have been concentrated in one squadron of the 321st Bomb Wing at McCoy AFB, Florida, and this unit carried out operational trials with the weapon in 1958, having received some modified DB-47s.

On 29 November 1958, however, the Rascal programme was cancelled by HQ USAF in deference to a far more promising air-launched missile system, the North American GAM-77 Hound Dog. This forty-three-foot missile had small canard fore-planes, a rear-mounted delta wing fitted with ailerons, a small fin and rudder, a very slim fuselage and a 7,500 lb s.t. Pratt & Whitney J52-6 turbojet in an underslung rear pod. The missile was designed to carry a one-megaton warhead over a range of between 500 and 700 miles, depending on the mission profile, and could operate between tree-top level and 55,000 feet at speeds of up to 2.1 M. The weapon was fitted with a North American Autonetics Division inertial system, which was

linked to the aircraft's navigation systems and continually updated by a Kollsman astro-tracker in the launch pylon.

The first powered test vehicle was launched from a converted B-52D over the Gulf Test Range on 23 April 1959, and on 23 December that year the first missile was handed over to the 4135th Strategic Wing (SW) at Eglin AFB, Florida. This unit, armed with B-52Gs – the Stratofortress variant designed to carry two Hound Dogs slung under its wings – was responsible for supporting Category III Hound Dog trials in co-ordination with Air Research and Development Command's Air Proving Ground Center, leading to SAC acceptance of the weapon system. The first SAC Hound Dog launch was made by a B-52G of the 4135th SW on 29 February 1960.

All B-52Gs and, later, B-52Hs armed with the Hound Dog carried one pylon-mounted round under each wing. The Hound Dogs' turbojets were lit up during take-off, effectively making the B-52 a ten-engined aircraft, and were subsequently shut down, the missile's tanks being topped up from the parent aircraft. After launch, the missile could follow a high or low flight profile, with dog-legs and diversions as necessary. Later, anti-radar and terrain contour matching (TERCOM) modifications were introduced. At the missile's peak in 1962 there were 592 Hound Dogs on SAC's inventory, and it is a measure of the system's effectiveness that it remained in operational service until 1976.

The urgent IA-PVO requirement for an aircraft capable of intercepting Strategic Air Command B-52s before they reached their missile launch points led directly to the development of the Tu-28 long-range, missile-armed all-weather interceptor, first seen by western observers at the Tushino air display of 1961. With a length of eighty-five feet and a wing span of sixty-five feet, the Tu-28, which was given the code-name *Fiddler*, was the largest interceptor to see service anywhere, and Western experts noted with interest, after they had gathered more intelligence on the aircraft, that its designation carried the suffix 'P' for *Perekhvachnik* (interceptor). The interesting point was that this suffix was only applied to the designations of Soviet aircraft which had been adapted to the fighter role, indicating that the Tu-28 had originally been designed as a low-level strike aircraft, possibly in the anti-shipping role. The Tu-28 was estimated to have a combat radius of around 1,500 miles with maximum fuel, and it was armed with four AA-5 Ash air-to-air missiles on underwing pylons.

The long-range Tu-28 was complemented by a series of medium-range fighters, products of the Sukhoi design bureau, which effectively formed a second barrier of defence. These were the Su-9/11 *Fishpot* and the larger twin-engined Su-15 *Flagon*.

The latter achieved brief notoriety in September 1983, when one destroyed a Korean Airlines Boeing 747 at night off Sakhalin Island, probably because Soviet air defence controllers had confused the airliner with an RC-135 reconnaissance aircraft that was in the vicinity.

Canada, forming the first line of defence against the threat of bombers attacking the North American continent across the great wastes of the Arctic, was quick to identify the need for a long-range night and all-weather interceptor during the early post-war years. In response to this requirement, Avro Canada designed the CF-100, at that time the largest fighter aircraft in the world. The prototype CF-100 Mk 1 flew on 19 January 1950, powered by two Rolls-Royce Avon RA3 turbojets; production aircraft were fitted with the Avro Orenda.

In September 1950 an order was placed with Avro Canada for 124 CF-100 Mk 3s for the RCAF. These were powered by two Orenda Mk 8s and armed with eight 0.5 in Colt-Browning machine-guns. In fact only seventy were built, the first entering service with No 445 Squadron. The next production version was the Mk 4A, powered by two

Orenda 9s and equipped with a Hughes AGP-40 fire control radar. This variant could be armed with forty-eight 'Mighty Mouse' high velocity aircraft rockets (HVAR), eight 0.5 in machine-guns or four 30 mm cannon in a ventral pack, plus fifty-eight HVAR rockets in wingtip pods. The first

Top and above: *The Convair F-102 all-weather interceptor's design was based on the XF-92 research aircraft, pictured here.* (Author)

production Mk 4A flew on 24 October 1953 and the aircraft entered service with No 445 Squadron in the following year. In all, 510 Mk 4As and 4Bs (the latter with Orenda 11 engines) were built, and by the end of 1957 nine RCAF squadrons were operating the type, providing round-the-clock air defence coverage of Canada's far north. Four CF-100 squadrons also served in Germany as part of Canada's NATO commitment, and fifty-three examples of the last production version, the Mk 5, were delivered to Belgium.

The CF-100 was to have been replaced in RCAF service by the very advanced Avro Canada CF-105 Arrow delta-wing interceptor, which flew for the first time on 25 March 1958, powered by two Pratt & Whitney J75 turbojets. Four more aircraft were built, designated CF-105 Mk 1, and four more – designated Mk 2, with 22,000 lb thrust Orenda PS-13 engines – were almost complete when the project was cancelled in February 1959. The Arrow was to have been armed with eight Sparrow AAMs.

In 1950, the USAF formulated a requirement for a night and all-weather interceptor incorporating the latest fire control system. This was eventually to emerge as the Convair F-102, whose design was based on experience gained during flight testing of the XF-92 delta-wing research aircraft. Two prototype YF-102s were built, the first flying on 24 October 1953. This aircraft was damaged beyond repair only a week later, but testing resumed with the second machine in January 1954. Eight more YF-102s were built for evaluation, and it soon became apparent that the aircraft's performance fell short of expectations. After substantial airframe redesign the machine re-emerged in December 1954 as the YF-102A, and the type was ordered into full production. The first F-102A was handed over to Air Defense Command in June 1955, but it was another year before the type was issued to squadrons.

In the interim, Air Defense Command had acquired an aircraft that went a long way to solving the problem of accurate interception at night and in bad weather. This was the North American F-86D, an aircraft bold in concept. Not only did the design envisage the replacement of the traditional interceptor armament of cannon or machine-guns by air-to-air missiles; it also envisaged that a single pilot would control the whole weapons system. Admittedly, the original F-86D design, begun in May 1948, had involved a two-seater aircraft, with a second crew member assisting the pilot in making radar-controlled interceptions and being responsible for navigation, but the performance limitations imposed by the installation of a second crew position – coupled with other attendant problems such as restricted fuselage fuel tank space – led to this concept being reconsidered. In the end, it was the availability of improved automated AI radar, reducing the operator's workload, that tipped the scales in favour of the single-seater.

Engineering design work on the single-seat F-86D was begun on 28 March 1949. The USAF showed an immediate interest in the project, and on 7 April work was started on the production version, the NA-165, and North American started building a mock-up in June.

The first of two YF-86D prototypes went to Muroc on 28 November 1949 and flew for the first time on 22 December. Much of the early test flying involved the evaluation of the electronic control system fitted to the afterburning General Electric J47-GE-17. At an early stage in the aircraft's design, it had been realised that pilots would find difficulty in monitoring the engine behaviour, especially during an AI radar intercept requiring the use of afterburner, so to overcome this problem North American and General Electric joined forces to develop a complex engine control system for installation in production F-86Ds. This involved the use of a single throttle lever control which, by means of an electronic fuel selector, determined the amount of fuel being supplied to the engine and afterburner to maintain maximum efficiency, even when the throttle was slammed open and shut rapidly.

Both YF-86Ds were flown without the fire control system, which was still under development by the Hughes Aircraft Corporation. The prototype system, the 50-kilowatt E-3, was approved by the Air Materiel Command on 17 February 1950 and was delivered to North American on 26 May; after some changes, it was installed in the second YF-86D and tested in September. The test programme was delayed when the YF-86D was damaged at Edwards Air Force Base (as Muroc was now known) as the result of an undercarriage malfunction, resuming on 17 October 1950.

The E-3 fire control system was installed in the first thirty-seven production F-86Ds pending delivery of the more complex 250-kW E-4, but even at this stage delays began to beset the programme. It was not until July 1951 that the first production E-3 system was delivered to NAA, and since aircraft could not be accepted for service without the system, it was October 1952 – three years after the original letter contract – that the USAF took delivery of the last of its thirty-seven F-86D-1s.

The situation with the E-4 system was just as bad, if not worse. The first set was delivered in December 1951, three months behind schedule, and was found to have a power output of only 180 kW instead of the planned 250. The first batch all suffered serious malfunctions, mostly because of extremely poor quality control at the manufacturer's works. Components were wired incorrectly or were of the wrong type, and foreign objects such as screwdrivers were found in the systems' innards. The upshot was that some systems had to be returned to the sub-contractors for repair, and for eleven modifications demanded by the USAF. At one time, in the winter of 1952–3, there were more than 320 F-86Ds awaiting the installation of the E-4 system and other electronic components.

Meanwhile, aerodynamic flight testing had revealed a number of problems created by changes of design from the original F-86A. The wing of the F-86D was generally similar to that of the F-86A, except that it was strengthened; the fuselage was dimensionally larger, the vertical tail surfaces were increased in area and a slab-type tailplane adopted for improved longitudinal control. The most noticeable external change was the design of the nose, which now featured a lowered nose intake topped by a 30 in fibreglass radome housing the antenna of the Hughes AN/APG search radar.

The F-86D's innovative weapons system also produced some teething troubles, all of which contributed to the slippage of the production programme. Early problems with the F-86D's armament, which comprised twenty-four 2.75 in folding fin aircraft rockets (FFAR) mounted in a retractable ventral pack, lay in its electronic linkage with the fire control system.

The weapons system was designed to work as follows. On a typical air defence mission beginning with a cold start, the F-86D would be off the ground in about four minutes, which included warming up time, and would then take eleven minutes to climb to 45,000 feet at full power. The pilot would then initiate the search phase, the AN/APG-36 (AN/APG-37 in later models) radar antenna sweeping an area 68.5 degrees left and right of the centreline in a three-and-a-half second cycle and also, if required, 33.5 degrees up and 13.5 degrees down. When a target was acquired at a range of up to thirty miles the radar locked on to it and the AN/APA-84 computer then worked out a lead collision course, which the pilot followed by keeping the 'blip' on his radar scope inside a one-inch circle.

When the automatic tracking system indicated twenty seconds to go, the system instructed the pilot to turn on to a 90-degree collision course, at which point he elected to launch six, twelve or all twenty-four rockets and pressed the trigger switch. The computer controlled the actual firing, extending the rocket pack in half a second and initiating the firing sequence when the target was about 500 yards away. It took only one-fifth of a second to fire the full salvo of rockets, each weighing eighteen pounds, the missiles fanning out like a charge of shotgun pellets to make sure of a hit. The rocket pack retracted in just over three seconds, and a symbol on the radar scope, which illuminated at a range of 250 yards, warned the pilot to break off.

Launching a full rocket salvo presented few problems; these tended to arise when the pilot selected a ripple-firing sequence, a procedure that saw frequent malfunctions. The system was updated and refined, but by the time the snags were ironed out the programme had slipped by two years, and it was

During the 1950s and early '60s, France made a valuable contribution to NATO's night and all-weather air defences with the Sud-Aviation Vautour IIN, pictured here. The type equipped the 6e and 30e Escadres de Chasse. (Philip Jarrett)

Meteor NF11s taking part in the Royal Review of the Royal Air Force at RAF Odiham in 1953 (Philip Jarrett)

A fine echelon formation by the Meteor NF12s of No 25 Squadron. The NF12 was a progressive development of the NF11, having a 17 in longer nose housing a US-built APS-21 AI radar. (Philip Jarrett)

not until April 1953 that the F-86D began to enter service with active Air Defense Command units. Thereafter, deliveries proceeded rapidly, and by the end of 1953 600 F-86Ds were in service with Air Defense Command. Eighteen months later, 1,026 – seventy-three per cent – of the Command's 1,405 interceptors were F-86Ds serving with the USAF overseas; some were assigned to the Fifth AF in Korea late in 1953, but the 'Sabre-Dog' was a much heavier fighter than the standard F-86 and it did not take kindly to operations from the still fairly primitive South Korean airfields. It was withdrawn after only a brief period of service in the peninsula. However, F-86Ds did equip the 199th Fighter

Interceptor Squadron of the 154th Fighter Group, Hawaiian Air National Guard, until they were replaced by Convair F-102A Delta Daggers in the early 1960s.

F-86Ds also served in the United Kingdom, equipping the 406th Fighter Wing (512th, 513th and 514th Fighter Interceptor Squadrons) at RAF Manston from November 1953. They provided a much-needed boost to the UK night and all-weather air defences, which were reliant on six squadrons of Meteor NF11s and two of Vampire NF10s. Two Meteor NF11 squadrons, Nos 68 and 87, were based in Germany, at Laarbruch and Wahn respectively, and in addition to their main

130

The last and most elegant Meteor of all, the NF14 equipped ten RAF squadrons. The aircraft pictured here in 1955 bear the markings of No 264 Squadron. (Philip Jarrett)

role of high-level defence they also trained for low-level defence and for night intruder operations, the latter involving night attacks on airfields, troop and armour concentrations. In the low-level air defence role their opponents were usually the A-26 Invaders of the USAF's 38th Bomb Group (Tactical) at Laon. The Meteor night fighter crews found these aircraft difficult targets, as many of the A-26s had served in the night intruder role in Korea and carried specialised night optics which enabled them to detect the attacking fighters at considerable ranges.

In November 1952 a new night fighter appeared on RAF Fighter Command's inventory. This was the de Havilland Venom NF2, the prototype of

which, like its Vampire NF10 precursor, had been produced as a private venture at the company's own expense. The first and only squadron to equip with the new aircraft, which was fitted with the AI Mk X, was No 23 at Coltishall, for after a number of crashes in 1954 the unit's aircraft were grounded for structural modifications, and the squadron did not become fully operational until the summer of that year.

Further modifications were carried out, and in the spring of 1955 the first of the modified aircraft, designated Venom NF2a, entered service with No 253 Squadron at Waterbeach. Venom NF2as were also issued to Nos 33 and 219 Squadrons, and the three squadrons formed an important element in

The de Havilland Venom NF3 equipped five RAF night fighter squadrons, in some cases replacing the Meteor NF11. (Philip Jarrett)

The de Havilland DH110 was in direct competition with the Gloster Javelin for a new RAF night/all-weather jet fighter. (Author)

Fighter Command's expanding night/all-weather fighter force. Ninety aircraft were built, the NF2a being followed into service by the NF3, which had the improved AI Mk 21 radar; this mark equipped Nos 23, 89, 125, 141 and 151 Squadrons.

The shortcomings of the RAF's night fighter force, meanwhile, had been demonstrated time and again by its inability, during air exercises, to get to grips with high-flying Canberra jet bombers. The Venom, which had an excellent high altitude performance, could intercept Canberras at up to 43,000 feet, but the Meteor NF11 had little chance. Indeed, on many occasions NF11 crews suffered the ignominy of having a Canberra turning the tables on them at high altitude and claiming them as its victim.

Both of the aircraft that Fighter Command was eagerly awaiting to replace its Meteor and Venom night fighters, the Gloster Javelin – designed as the GA5 to Specification F4/48 – and its direct competitor, the de Havilland DH110, had suffered serious misfortunes during their development careers. De Havilland's swept-wing, twin-boom DH110 flew for the first time on 26 September 1951, powered by two Rolls-Royce Avons, and six months into the test programme, on 9 April 1952, this aircraft (WG236) became the first twin-engined two-seater to exceed Mach 1.0 in a dive. The second DH110 prototype, WG240, flew on 25 July 1952. Painted a rather sinister all-black, WG240 was demonstrated by test pilot John Derry at that year's Farnborough air show on every day except 6 September, when it went unserviceable. Derry switched to the other DH110, WG236, and went into his usual display routine. He was pulling a high G turn about a mile outside the airfield perimeter when the aircraft broke up without warning as a

result of the structural failure of the starboard outer wing section. The results were catastrophic; Derry and his observer were killed and debris plunged into the crowd, causing many fatalities and injuries.

The second prototype DH110 was grounded as a result of this tragic accident, and in 1953 the RAF decided to fill its night/all-weather requirement with the Gloster Javelin. Yet in many respects, the DH110 was the better design; it was certainly more manoeuvrable, its handling qualities comparing closely with those of many smaller single-seat fighters, and it was very stable in a high G turn right down to the stall, which the Javelin was not. Nevertheless, de Havilland resumed testing with the second DH110 after further structural modifications, with a naval requirement in mind, and in September 1953 it undertook carrier trials aboard HMS *Albion*. A production order for a developed naval version followed, and this eventually entered Fleet Air Arm service as the Sea Vixen F(AW)1 – an aircraft which, for the first time, gave the Royal Navy a true round-the-clock all-weather fighter capability.

Construction of the prototype Gloster GA5, the world's first twin-jet delta and an extremely radical design for its day, began in April 1949, and the aircraft (WD804) flew for the first time on 26 November 1951, powered by two 7,000 lb thrust Armstrong-Siddeley Sapphires. The maiden flight was attended by a serious snag in the shape of rudder buffeting, and further flight testing was delayed while modifications were carried out. Then, on 29 June 1952, the protoype lost both elevators and was destroyed in a crash landing at Boscombe Down. (The test pilot, Squadron Leader W.A. Waterton, was subsequently awarded the George Medal for his action in retrieving the vital

Line-up of Gloster Javelins of No 46 Squadron, the first to receive the type. (Philip Jarrett)

flight recorder from the blazing wreckage).

Testing continued with the second prototype, WD808, which flew on 21 August 1952, but this aircraft was also destroyed on 11 June 1953 as the result of a super-stall condition. Three more prototypes had been ordered in the meantime: the third aircraft (WT827) flew on 7 March 1953 and carried an armament of four 30 mm cannon, while the fourth featured a modified wing shape and the fifth, which flew on 20 July 1954, was up to full production standard, with British AI Mk 17 radar.

As the Javelin FAW1, the new fighter was ordered into 'super-priority' production for the RAF. The first production aircraft flew on 22 July 1954 and deliveries began to No 46 Squadron at RAF Odiham in February 1956. Javelin FAW1s were also issued to No 87 Squadron, which formed part of 2nd TAF in Germany. In October 1955 a new variant, the Javelin FAW2, made its appearance; this was basically similar to the FAW1 apart from its radar, which was the American-designed AI22 (APQ43) and avionics, and replaced the earlier production model in No 56 Squadron.

Next on the production line was the FAW4, the prototype of which was the 41st FAW1 with an all-moving tailplane. This variant entered service with No 141 Squadron early in 1957, and except for the tailplane was essentially similar to the FAW1. Later that year, No 151 Squadron received the first examples of the Javelin FAW5, which had a modified wing structure and increased internal fuel capacity, and in 1958 the Javelin FAW6 – which was basically an FAW5 with the same radar as the FAW2 –

entered service with No 89 Squadron.

In November 1956 the Javelin's already formidable combat potential was given an extra boost with the appearance of the FAW7, which was fitted with Sapphire ASSa7R turbojets developing 12,300 lb thrust with reheat in place of the 8,300 lb thrust Sapphire ASSa6 engines used in earlier marks. The Javelin FAW7, which incorporated further structural modifications and increased wing fuel tankage, had an armament of two 30 mm ADEN cannon and four Firestreak AAMs. It entered service with No 33 Squadron at RAF Leeming in July 1958. The FAW8, which flew on 9 May 1958, was externally similar to the FAW7; it incorporated the US Mk 22 radar, a simplified afterburning system, a Sperry autopilot, drooped wing leading edges and dampers on the yaw and pitch axes. The FAW8 was the last production model of the Javelin, the final aircraft being completed in June 1960, but a number of Javelin FAW7s were brought up to FAW8 standard (although with British AI radar) and designated FAW9.

The Javelin, which at various stages in its service career equipped sixteen RAF squadrons at home and overseas, was a vital component in NATO's European night and all-weather air defence system. It helped to pioneer a number of night fighting techniques, one of which was a mixed night fighter force of Javelins and Hunters, the former leading the latter to the target in a way not unreminiscent of the Havoc-Hurricane-Defiant combination of 1941–2. The technique was tested by Nos 33 and 92 Squadrons at RAF Middleton St George in the late

133

Javelin FAW9s of No 29 Squadron, armed with Firestreak AAMs. (Philip Jarrett)

1950s and was quite successful unless large numbers of aircraft were operating, when it was less so.

In the early 1960s the Javelin was progressively replaced in the air defence role by the English Electric Lightning, while the USAF's night and all-weather interceptor force's F-102s and F-106s were supplanted by the McDonnell F-4 Phantom, an aircraft that would also see RAF service in the interceptor role. The day of the dedicated night/all-weather fighter was fast approaching its end: the interceptor capable of operating round the clock, in all weathers, armed with air-to-air missiles capable of killing targets at extreme radar range – far beyond the limits of the human eye – was on the horizon.

But there was still a night battle to be fought, with methods not far removed from those of Korea and the closing stages of World War II; but the battleground was far removed from the unpredictable skies of Europe.

CHAPTER FIFTEEN

LAST BATTLES

When USAF and USN fighter-bombers began attacking targets in North Vietnam in August 1964, any doubts the crews may have harboured about the capability of the small North Vietnamese Air Force (NVAF) were soon dispelled. The NVAF's most numerous type, the MiG-17, proved to be a serious threat to the much heavier, bomb-laden F-4s and F-105s, while the MiG-21 could match the latest American types in every respect except quality of weapons and avionics.

Neither the MiG-17 nor the MiG-21 were specialised night fighters, but they often operated in that capacity, particularly when the American night bombing campaign against the North intensified during 1972. One USN pilot, Captain R.E. Tucker, recalled that:

'During 1972, when Navy A-6s were making a number of single aircraft low-level night strikes all over the area between Haiphong and Hanoi, MiGs were known to launch, making the A-6 drivers nervous (although I personally felt that the MiGs had no night/IFR capability against an A-6 at 300 feet). As a result, we started positioning a single F-4 on MIGCAP along the coastline at night. We figured a single F-4 didn't have to worry about a mid-air with his wingman and had plenty of potential at night against a single MiG. If a MiG launched and headed towards an A-6, the F-4 would vector for the MiG. Invariably MiGs would run for home when the F-4 got to within 25–30 miles of them. Some pilots weren't too overjoyed about the night MIGCAP missions, but I personally felt it was a golden opportunity and my MiG kill proved it. I figured that the MiG had a negligible opportunity to do anyone bodily harm at night with his limited weapons system and Atoll/guns load, whereas the F-4 had a good solid head-on or tail shot against any MiG he could find and get close enough to shoot at.'

Tucker, then a Lieutenant-Commander, was flying an F-4 Phantom of VF-103, operating from the USS *Saratoga*, when he destroyed a MiG-21 on 10/11 August 1972. The Phantom was armed with two AIM-7E Sparrows and two AIM-9D Sidewinders.

Tucker was refuelling from a KA-6D tanker when he heard the fighter controller vector another Phantom on to a MiG. He immediately broke contact and joined the other F-4 in the search, the controller advising him that the enemy aircraft was at 8,000 feet, 140 degrees at twelve miles range. Tucker descended to 8,000 feet and his RIO, Lieutenant (JG) Bruce Edens, got a radar contact at once. Lighting his afterburners, Tucker accelerated to 650 knots and closed to within five miles of the MiG, at which point Edens advised the pilot that he had lost radar contact. Realising that the MiG pilot had probably descended, Tucker went down to 3,500 feet; Edens announced that he had regained contact and that the MiG was seven or eight miles ahead.

Tucker jettisoned his centreline fuel tanks and accelerated to 750 knots, overtaking the MiG from directly astern. At a range of about two miles he launched two Sparrows, the second one leaving the under-fuselage rack just as the first warhead detonated. Tucker reported:

'There was a large fireball, and the second missile impacted in the same spot. I came right slightly to avoid any debris. The target on our radar appeared to stop in mid-air and within a second or two the radar broke lock. The MiG-21 pilot did not survive. If he ejected after the first missile, the second missile must have done him in. We couldn't see any debris in the dark ... The kill was confirmed about three days later.'

In May and June 1972, B-52 bombers ventured into heavily defended North Vietnamese airspace for the first time to make limited night attacks on airfields and oil storage facilities, and also to lay mines in the waters of Haiphong and other strategic ports. These minelaying operations, carried out by modified B-52Ds, were also flown under cover of darkness, and no losses were sustained.

On 20 October 1972, when it seemed as though peace talks in Paris were at last leading to an agreement that would end the war, air operations over North Vietnam were once more halted. They were resumed when the peace talks again broke down amid indications that the North Vietnamese were preparing to renew their offensive in the

Top and above: *B-52D bombers operating from Guam and Thailand carried out an intensive campaign against North Vietnam in December 1952, and suffered heavy losses – but to surface-to-air missiles, not night fighters.* (Philip Jarrett)

south. There followed an eleven-day bombing campaign against the north which developed into the heaviest bombing offensive of the war, with round-the-clock attacks on targets which had mostly been on the restricted list until then. They included rail yards, power plants, communications facilities, petrol, oil and lubrication (POL) stores and ammunition supply dumps, as well as the principal North Vietnamese Air Force fighter bases and SAM sites. The target list numbered thirty-four strategic objectives, over sixty per cent of which were situated within a twenty-five-mile radius of Hanoi.

The original plan called for the B-52s to attack at night, in three waves, with F-111s and A-6s continuing the offensive in daylight. The B-52 bomber streams were to be preceded by F-111

interdictors, attacking fighter bases at low level, and F-4 Phantoms dropping *Window* – still a very effective countermeasure, thirty years after it was first used in the Battle of Hamburg.

The B-52s were to approach their target areas from the north-west, using strong high-altitude winds to give them a much increased ground speed, and after bomb release they were to swing away from the target in tight turns in order to clear SAM defences as quickly as possible. Attacks would be made by cells of three aircraft, generally bombing from 33,000 feet. The three aircraft were to fly in close formation to pool their ECM resources, which included the GE ALQ-87 and ITT ALQ-117 jammers and the Lundy ALE-24 chaff dispensing system. In fact, the B-52D was better equipped with ECM than SAC's main force B-52Gs, some of which were brought in to augment the bombing force during *Linebacker* II.

The operation began on 18/19 December 1972, when 129 B-52s took off from their respective bases in Thailand and on Guam. Thirty minutes before the first cells arrived over their targets, F-111s carried out strikes on enemy airfields and F-4s sowed two chaff corridors to screen the attacks on the target areas of Kinh No and Yen Vien, north of Hanoi. Unfortunately, the strong north-west wind had dispersed the chaff before the B-52s arrived.

The first B-52 wave to attack the Yen Vien rail yards flew over a cluster of SAM sites as it began its final run-in to the target, and Charcoal 1 – the leading aircraft in the 'Charcoal' cell – sustained a near miss from an SA-2 just as its bomb doors were opening. Crippled and out of control, with its pilot, co-pilot and gunner either dead or incapacitated, the bomber began its long plunge to earth. The navigator, radar navigator and electronic warfare officer ejected and were taken prisoners. A second B-52, attacking with 'Peach' cell in the second wave four hours later, was luckier; it was also crippled by an SA-2, this time just after completing its bombing run, but managed to reach friendly territory with wing and engine fires before its crew were forced to abandon it.

The third wave of eighteen B-52s, attacking five hours later, encountered fierce opposition over the target (the Hanoi railway repair shops). More than sixty SAM launches were observed, but the bombers' ECM worked well and there were no losses, although one aircraft was damaged by a near miss. Another wave of twenty-one aircraft, attacking from the west, also encountered heavy opposition from eleven SAM sites in the Hanoi area and lost the leading aircraft in the last cell to bomb, Rose 1. On this first night of *Linebacker* II, therefore, in which the enemy had launched more than 200 SAMs and expended massive quantities of AAA ammunition, the SA-2s had destroyed three B-52s and damaged three more. The situation might have been much worse, because the MiGs were up in strength, but the Phantom MIGCAP kept them at arm's length and they achieved no successes.

The B-52s suffered no casualties on 19/20 December, when 120 bombers attacked several targets in the Hanoi area. However, the North Vietnamese had by now realised that the bombers were approaching their target areas along the same tracks each night, and they evolved new tactics that included sending up MiGs to shadow the incoming bomber stream and verify its altitude, so that the defences could fuse their missile warheads and AAA shells accordingly.

During the third night of operations, on 20/21 December, SA-2s knocked down two B-52s as they completed their bombing runs, and both of them crashed in Hanoi. A third B-52, badly damaged, struggled back to Thailand, only to crash on landing, killing four of its crew. Two more B-52s in the last wave that night were destroyed by SAMs; a third was crippled and crashed in Laos. In the nine-hour operation the enemy had fired 220 SAMs and claimed six B-52s, four of which were B-52Gs.

On the fourth night, 21/22 December, the tactics employed by the bomber stream were modified. The time between attacking waves was greatly reduced, attacking altitudes were varied and the cells were randomly spaced. In addition, individual crews were given freedom of action in evasive manoeuvring; most favoured a shallow post-attack turn followed by a dive to low altitude and a high-speed run clear of the Vietnamese defences over the Gulf of Tonkin. All sorties on this night were flown from U-Tapao, the Guam-based B-52s being released for *Arc Light* missions (carpet-bombing attacks on suspected NVA troop movements in the south) and there were no losses.

The B-52 force was stood down for thirty-six hours over the Christmas period, but on 26/27 December 120 B-52s, flying in tightly compressed waves and accompanied by 113 defence suppression and ECM aircraft, attacked ten targets in Hanoi, Haiphong and Thai Nguyen, the more vulnerable B-52Gs being assigned to the latter objectives. Two streams attacked Hanoi from the north-west, flying in from Laos and out over the Gulf of Tonkin, while two more attacked on a reciprocal track. All the bombers passed through the target areas within fifteen minutes and only one B-52 fell to the SAM defences, although a second, severely damaged, crashed short of the runway while attempting to land at U-Tapao in Thailand.

The last three nights of *Linebacker* II, in which sixty B-52s were committed on each night, cost SAC five more bombers, all victims of SAMs. By this time the North Vietnamese defences had been virtually neutralised, and the enemy had expended most of their stock of about 1,000 SA-2s. On 30 December, North Vietnam announced that it was ready to resume peace negotiations.

In all, 729 B-52 sorties had been flown during *Linebacker* II, and more than 15,000 tons of bombs dropped out of a total of 20,370 tons. Fifteen B-52s had been lost to the SAM defences, and nine damaged. Thirty-four targets had been hit, and some 1,500 civilians killed. Of the ninety-two crew members aboard the shot-down bombers, twenty-six were recovered by rescue teams, twenty-nine were listed as missing, and thirty-three baled out over North Vietnam to be taken prisoner and later repatriated.

Compared with the threat from North Vietnam's SA-2 *Guideline* surface-to-air missiles, the threat from night fighters and AAA had been small during the eleven nights of *Linebacker* II. On the first night of the operation, a MiG-21 was shot down in a radar-directed gun engagement by Staff Sergeant Samuel O. Turner, the tail gunner in a B-52D; and a second MiG was destroyed by B-52 gunners before the brief campaign was over.

These were the last occasions in the history of air warfare when attacking night fighters were destroyed by a bomber's defensive gunfire.

CHAPTER SIXTEEN

FROM NIGHT FIGHTER TO STRATEGIC FIGHTER

For the former Soviet Air Defence Forces – which had to cope with the threat of air attack from virtually any direction – the deployment of strategic interceptors in considerable numbers around the country's vast periphery was of paramount importance during the years of the Cold War. The first of them, as we have seen, was the Tupolev Tu-28.

The United States Air Force, on the other hand, faced a threat of attack by manned bombers flying over the Arctic, and was consequently able to place its strategic fighter defences well forward, in Alaska, Greenland and Iceland. For many years, the front line was held by the Convair F-102A Delta Dagger and its development, the F-106 Delta Dart, armed with the Douglas AIR-2 Genie or Super Genie nuclear-tipped AAM. These older aircraft were later replaced by the F-4 Phantom and, ultimately, the F-15 Eagle.

Although the Soviet-manned strategic bomber threat was never particularly great at the height of the Cold War – the Soviet leadership having opted instead for the development of advanced strategic missiles – it was revived in the latter years with the deployment of a version of the Tu-95 Bear armed with cruise missiles and of the Tu-160 Blackjack supersonic variable-geometry bomber, the broad equivalent of America's B-1.

America's principal NATO partner, Britain, also faced an air threat from one main axis, but the British air defences had to expect a much shorter warning time. It was therefore imperative to deploy an aircraft with a rapid reaction time, and in this respect the BAC Lightning was excellent. With the aircraft off the ground interception was a fairly straightforward matter, even though the main medium between pilot and controller was voice communication. (It had always been intended that the Lightning be equipped with a datalink for the passage of data from a ground-based computer to the aircraft's auto-attack system, but this was never fitted.) In a rear-sector attack with the Lightning's Firestreak AAM missiles the target would have been well within visual range during the final stage, provided it was daytime, so there was little danger of engaging a friendly aircraft.

The replacement of the Lightning by the McDonnell Douglas Phantom FG1/FGR2 brought about some dramatic changes in the RAF's Rules of Engagement, because the Phantom carried an impressive array of weapons, including some with a genuine 'beyond visual range' capability, and this raised many issues of identification, classification and tactics which had to be solved by tighter controls and realistic training if the risk of a costly error was to be eliminated. The AIM-7 Sparrow was capable of engaging targets at ranges well in excess of twelve miles, and at that distance the foolproof identification of a target without some form of visual enhancement was virtually impossible. The Phantom entered full RAF service in the air defence role without any aid to visual identification, although US variants had carried an electro-optical device for this purpose for some time. The British variant was eventually fitted with air-to-air IFF, radar warning sensors and a telescope system.

Principally, the RAF's air defence system had to guard against attacks by a new generation of fast Soviet aircraft armed with long-range missiles, which generated a requirement for an interceptor capable of spending lengthy periods on patrol on the axis of the potential air threat, a long way from its home bases. At the beginning of the 1970s the Lightning was reaching the end of its useful life and its systems left a lot to be desired, while the Phantom, although expected to fulfil the air defence role adequately, would need to be phased out in favour of a more advanced weapons system in the late 1980s.

In 1971, therefore, the Ministry of Defence issued Air Staff Target 395, which called for a minimum-change, minimum-cost but effective interceptor to replace the British Aerospace Lightning and the F-4 Phantom in the air defence of the United Kingdom. Primary armament was to be the British Aerospace Dynamics XJ521 Sky Flash medium-range air-to-air missile, and the primary sensor a Marconi Avionics pulse-Doppler radar. The result was the Air Defence Variant (ADV) of the Panavia Tornado interdictor/strike (IDS), an aircraft that provides a good illustration of a modern round-the-clock interceptor and its

140 Top and above: *The English Electric (BAC) Lightning gave RAF Fighter Command a round-the-clock defensive capability, replacing the Hunter and Javelin in their respective day and night roles.* (Philip Jarrett)

The Phantom was the first RAF aircraft to be armed with missiles that could hit targets beyond visual range. (RAF)

associated systems.

The original Tornado ADV study envisaged four Sky Flash missiles under the wings, long-range tanks under the fuselage and a modified nose to accommodate the AI radar. Early aerodynamic trials, however, showed that with pylon-mounted missiles the ADV's performance fell short of requirements, giving little or no advantage over the Phantom it was intended to replace, even allowing for further engine developments. The answer was to carry the AAMs semi-submerged under the fuselage, providing a low-drag configuration. To accommodate the front pair of missiles some lengthening of the forward fuselage was necessary, but this produced an added bonus in that it increased internal fuel capacity by ten per cent. A further armament change involved the deletion of one of the ADV's two planned Mauser 27 mm cannon, providing more space for the installation of avionics. The overall structural changes involved stretching the fuselage by 53 in; the wing root glove was also given increased sweep, moving the centre of pressure forward to compensate for the resultant change of centre of gravity and to reduce wave drag.

Because of the minimum-change requirement, the only changes permitted to the Tornado IDS weapon system were those that would produce an effective air defence aircraft at minimum cost. First of all, this involved the removal of all equipment not required for the air defence role, including the Texas Instruments terrain-following/ground mapping radar. The next stage was to identify equipment that only required modification to

perform the air defence role. This included the Command Stability Augmentation System (CSAS), which required inputs to reduce stick pitch forces and increase roll rates for air combat. The result was a system common to both Tornado ADV and IDS, with the air defence equipment added. This comprised the Marconi Avionics AI radar, with integrated Cossor IFF interrogator, Singer-Kearfott secure datalink, Marconi Space and Defence Systems radar homing and warning receiver, Smiths Industries/Computing Devices missile management system, and a new electronic head-down display in the front cockpit. All this required a considerable re-write of the main computer software and resulted in more changes than had originally been envisaged. Each step was approved separately by the MoD, which considered a number of alternatives – including the F-14 and F-15 – before finally approving the whole ADV project in 1976.

The aircraft that eventually emerged was a long-range interceptor, with long on-CAP (Combat Air Patrol) time, capable of engaging multiple targets in rapid succession, in all weathers and in complex ECM conditions. It was designed to operate with the United Kingdom Air Defence Ground Environment (UKADGE), airborne early warning (AEW) aircraft, tankers and air defence ships, all linked in due course to a secure ECM-resistance data and voice command and control net. The problem of navigation at extreme range from fixed navigational systems was overcome by a highly accurate twin inertial platform, the Ferranti

141

Top and above: *The prototype Panavia Tornado Air Defence Variant (ADV) taking off from BAe Warton, Lancashire . . . and in a powerful climb out with reheat on.* (BAe)

FIN1010, which provided the computer with accurate position data for steering to a large number of fixed or moving positions. This could be done automatically by use of the autopilot, allowing the crew to concentrate on the tactical information provided by the AI radar and datalink.

The intercept radar selected for the Tornado ADV was the Marconi (later GEC Marconi) Avionics AI24 Foxhunter, development of which began in 1974. The essential requirement was that detection ranges should in no way be limited to target altitude. Look-down capability against low-level targets was the most demanding case, particularly when the interceptor itself was at low altitude. Severe and sophisticated electronic countermeasures also had to be overcome.

By the time the first Tornado ADV was ready to fly, late in 1979, the external stores fit had also undergone changes. The four Sky Flash AAMs were now joined by four AIM-9L Sidewinders on underwing stations, and the capacity of each drop tank increased from 1,500 litres to 2,250 litres to extend unrefuelled range and time on CAP.

Three Tornado ADV prototypes were built. All were powered by the Turbo-Union RB199 Mk 103 turbofan, which was also to power the initial production batch of Tornado F-2s for the RAF. These aircraft also featured manually-controlled wing sweep, which would be automatic on later production aircraft. The first development Tornado ADV, A01, was a single-stick aircraft assigned to handling, performance and general systems evaluation. Early in 1982, to demonstrate that the ADV could fulfil its CAP requirements in all respects, this aircraft flew a CAP of two hours twenty minutes over the North Sea, involving a flight of 325 nm to the CAP area and a similar return flight. The aircraft was climbed out of Warton, Lancashire, and cruised at high altitude over the North Sea, then descended to medium altitude to take up a CAP racetrack pattern. On arriving back at base the aircraft loitered in the local area for fifteen minutes at low level before landing with more than five per cent internal fuel remaining after a total flight time of four hours thirteen minutes.

It was a very promising indication of the ADV's capability. So were the armament trials, carried out by A02 in the same year. Sky Flash firings were carried out from 0.9 M into the supersonic envelope, while Mauser gun firing trials covered the subsonic flight envelope above 200 kt from zero G to the angle of attack limit, and up to 30,000 feet. By the end of 1982, A03 had done most of the necessary radar and weapon system integration flight trials and pre-production radar flight trials were scheduled to start in the near future, although it was now apparent that deliveries of the operational AI24 were going to be alarmingly late.

Despite problems with the AI radar there was nothing wrong with the aircraft and its other systems, and orders for the RAF now stood at 165, to be delivered in three batches. Pilots of 'A' Squadron of the Aeroplane and Armament Experimental Establishment (A&AEE) at Boscombe Down, who evaluated it, were very enthusiastic about all aspects except the radar, which failed to meet its specification in no fewer than fifty-two areas.

The problems with the Foxhunter were still far from resolved when the first Tornado F-2s were delivered to No 229 Operational Conversion Unit (OCU) at RAF Coningsby, in Lincolnshire, in November 1984. The first eighteen aircraft were all powered by Mk 103 engines; aircraft after that had the more powerful Mk 104, which combined a 360 mm reheat extension with a Lucas Aerospace digital electronic engine control unit (DECU). These later aircraft, designated Tornado F-3 – the definitive production version of the design – also featured the full armament of four Sky Flash and four AIM-9Ls, auto wing sweep, and automanoeuvre devices with the slats and flaps deploying as a function of angle of attack and wing sweep.

It was not until 1986 that the first modified AI24 Foxhunter radars were delivered for installation in the OCU aircraft, the necessary modifications having cost an additional £250 million. The first squadron, No 29, formed at RAF Coningsby in May 1987 and was declared operational at the end of November. The aircraft eventually armed seven squadrons in addition to No 229 OCU (which became No 56 Reserve Squadron on 1 July 1992).

The Tornado F-3 opened up a whole range of tactical possibilities for No 11 Group RAF, the air defence group responsible for its operations. Its excellent take-off and landing characteristics mean that the aircraft can, if necessary, deploy to small airfields or even sections of motorway, together with its Auxiliary Power Unit and datalink. All the crew needs to do is remain on cockpit alert, monitoring tactical developments on the multi-function displays via the datalink, and wait for the order to scramble. Long before combat is joined, pilot and navigator will have an accurate appraisal of the tactical situation.

Normal air defence operations with the Tornado F-3 involve what is known as a 'heavy combat fit', which means four Sky Flash, four Sidewinders and no external tanks. CAP fit with the two tanks is reserved specifically for long-range sorties. A good example of what the F-3 can achieve without the long-range tank was given on 10 September 1988, when two aircraft of No 5 Squadron were scrambled from RAF Coningsby to intercept a pair of Tupolev Tu-95 Bear-D maritime radar reconnaissance aircraft over the Norwegian Sea. A VC-10 tanker was scrambled from RAF Leuchars to rendezvous with the Tornados, which carried out the intercept successfully.

The Tornado F-3 is, first and foremost, a missile platform. The aircraft's AI24 radar uses a technique known as frequency modulated interrupted continuous wave (FMICW), with which is integrated a Cossor IFF-3500 interrogator and a radar signal processor to suppress ground clutter (which, in fact, was one of the major problems associated with its protracted development). The radar's high pulse repetition frequency (PRF) enables it to detect targets at an initial range of about 100 nm, while FMICW allows the range of the target to be determined from the frequency change between transmission and reception.

As they are detected, the targets are stored in the Central Digital Computer, which is the same as that in the Tornado IDS variant. Since the radar continues to scan normally, the targets are unaware that they are the subject of detailed analysis. The system rejects unwanted signals, leaving only real targets which then pass through the radar data processor prior to display to the aircraft's crew. While the radar keeps up a 'running commentary' on ranges, velocities and tracks of established targets, it continues to scan and report new plots. With the computer fully updated, the crew plan their approach to engage the maximum number of targets. Displays are duplicated in the front cockpit for the pilot, who steers to the engagement on his head-up display. The symbology for Sky Flash, Sidewinder or gun attacks is very clear, and an important feature is the target indicator which aids the pilot in an early visual sighting.

For a long-range interception, the Sky Flash semi-active radar homing AAM would be used. This weapon was developed from the AIM-7E Sparrow and features several areas of improvement, including early discrimination between grouped targets, positive target detection and tracking against ground radar clutter, ECM resistance, more accurate guidance resulting in reduced miss distance, better proximity fusing and improved reliability. The original version required continuous-wave illumination by the launch aircraft's radar all the way to the target, but the latest version is fitted with an MSDS monopulse radar homing head. It can engage targets at high altitude or down to 250 feet in the face of heavy ECM and at stand-off ranges of more than 25 nm.

The Sky Flash launch sequence lasts less than a tenth of a second, the missile being driven down from its fuselage recess by two gas-operated, long-stroke rams (developed by Frazer-Nash) through the flow fields around the aircraft. Additionally, the rams stabilise the missile in roll and yaw during ejection, and are then retracted to avoid adding

post-launch drag. The system enables the F-3 to launch its missiles across the entire flight envelope. The Tornado F-3 is also compatible with the AIM-120 Advanced Medium Range AAM (AMRAAM).

For engagements at closer range the AIM-9L infra-red homing AAM Sidewinder would be used. To respond quickly to a close-in threat, the pilot can take control of the weapons systems by selecting the air-to-air override mode. This mode, optimised for visual combat, is controlled by two multi-function buttons mounted on the throttle. Pressing the buttons in sequence selects the close combat radar mode and associated HUDs (Head-Up Display), as well as the required weapons, without the pilot having to take his hands off the throttle or stick. A hand controller, located aft of the throttles, may be used to slew the radar scanner or missile homing heads if the automatic HUD scan pattern is insufficient to acquire the target. Once the target is in scan, lock-on is automatic. The AIM-132 Advanced Short Range AAM (ASRAAM) is also integrated on the F-3.

Although not a fighter in the strictest sense of the word, the Tornado F-3 gives an excellent account of itself in combat with other contemporary aircraft, including the F-16 Fighting Falcon. With its wings swept at forty-five degrees the Tornado can hold its own in a turning fight with most combat aircraft of its generation. The aircraft's Spin Prevention and Incidence Limiting System (SPILS) provides care-free handling, and stick forces are about thirty per cent lighter than those of the Tornado GR1. Another useful feature is that the pilot can bang the throttles open and shut without penalty. The F-3 is capable of 2.2 M at high level, and more than 800 kt at low level; in both cases, fuel consumption is surprisingly low. A 'clean' Tornado F-3 can fly for one hour at 420 kt, low level, and still have enough fuel for half an hour's flying time.

No modern fighter, whether designed for air superiority over the battlefield or long-range interception, can function successfully without being fully integrated with airborne and ground-based electronic surveillance systems. Today's ground-based systems combine a centralised command structure with a decentralised sensor network that is secure, survivable and capable of functioning even after sustaining substantial damage. They are based on advanced portable ground radars, enabling sensors to be deployed almost anywhere, and telecommunications technology providing a network of lines and exchanges that would continue to route both voice and data transmissions along any path so long as some sort of physical connection remains.

The Improved United Kingdom Air Defence Ground Environment is typical of such a system. IUKADGE involves three different types of new-generation radar, operating in two wavebands. There are two General Electric GE592 and four

GEC/Marconi Martello 23 cm radars, operating in the L-band, and six Plessey/ITT 10 cm radars operating in the S-band. All are three-dimensional radars capable of measuring target range, bearing and height. Each radar is deployed in a convoy of about fifteen vehicles to a pre-surveyed but unmarked site indistinguishable from the surrounding countryside. The radar head is located remotely from its associated reporting post, and is protected by decoys intended to confuse anti-radar missiles. The overlapping L- and S-band coverage also reduces the risk of enemy jamming. As an extra insurance, an electronic counter-countermeasures officer forms part of the reporting post (RP) trailer crew, his function to assist the radar in overcoming any jamming problems.

Associated with four of the twelve RPs are hardened Command and Reporting Posts (CRPs) with local tracking and fighter control capability; these provide backup facilities for the Command and Reporting Centres (CRCs), which under normal circumstances are responsible for tracking and interceptor control and which are the nerve centres of the UK air defence system.

The process of building up a picture of a possible air threat begins with the first receipt of radar plots (target positions) and strobes (the bearings of enemy jammers). This information is fed into the air defence system via a narrow-band datalink. At the CRC, the plots are combined with those of other radars for multi-radar target tracking; these active tracks are then combined with passive tracks derived from jamming strobes. Tracks from airborne early warning (AEW) and interceptor aircraft are also introduced, together with those from other CRCs, and track-to-track correlation is carried out to produce the local picture. Then the recognition process begins, an automatic interface with the principal air traffic control centre ensuring instant access to all currently filed civil flight plans.

With the threat revealed, the fighter controllers can now marshal and direct their forces. Sea tracks are introduced into the system to produce the final recognised air-sea picture; this mutual exchange of information between elements ensures that all centres share the same constantly updated picture of the UK Air Defence Region (UKADR), so that even if an element is lost, the big picture will remain intact. In addition, the CRCs interface with the NATO Air Defence Ground Environment (NADGE) and France's STRIDA II air defence systems for target data exchange.

Another key element in the air defence system is the airborne early warning aircraft, and in this respect the NATO requirement is filled by the Boeing E-3 Sentry. The Boeing E-3, originally known as the EC-137, stemmed from a NATO requirement for an early warning aircraft equipped with radar systems capable of extending the low-altitude radar view of Warsaw Pact territory by as much as 150 miles, thereby filling the existing gaps in low-altitude coverage left by ground-based radars, and providing a major advance in early warning protection. Although the perceived threat from the east has receded over the horizon, if not vanished entirely, the core of the E-3's role today remains the detection of an air threat. Its primary function in the 1991 Gulf War was to detect the movement of Iraqi aircraft and to direct Allied fighters to the point where a successful interception could be made. It has been used extensively for surveillance of Bosnia (Operation *Deny Flight*), providing intelligence of aircraft, helicopter and missile battery movements that might present a threat to UN peacekeeping forces, and in directing NATO air attacks on targets in Serbia and Kosovo (Operation *Combined Force*).

At the heart of the E-3's systems is its Westinghouse surveillance radar, which can track targets more than 300 nm away while the E-3 orbits at 30,000 feet. The thirty-foot diameter radome turns at six revolutions per minute when the equipment is active, and has various operating modes depending on the task in hand. The standard E-3A's radar was later modified to track ships, and other modifications included the fitting of a faster central computer with expanded memory, together with improved communications equipment. This included the Joint Tactical Information Distribution System (JTIDS), which ensures an unbroken transmission of data if main communications links are disrupted and gives fighter and attack crews an unprecedented picture of the air battle. Fighters equipped with the system include the F-15 and Tornado F-3. The E-3 Sentry fulfils the Airborne Warning and Command System (AWACS) role with the USAF, the RAF and NATO, and with the French Air Force.

It is technology far removed from the primitive AI that led a Blenheim of the Fighter Interception Unit to the first radar-aided destruction of an enemy bomber, on that July night in 1940.

RAF NIGHT FIGHTER VICTORIES, JULY 1940–MAY 1941

Date	Enemy a/c	Unit	Attacking a/c	Unit	Remarks
23/24 July 1940	Do 17Z	2/KG3	Blenheim	FIU	Off Sussex
25/26 July 1940	He 111H-4	1/KG4	Hurricane	87 Sqn	Nr Honiton, Devon
11/12 August 1940	He 111H-3	2/KG27	Unknown		Nr Wimborne, Dorset
16/17 August 1940	Ju 88	4/NJG1	Blenheim	29 Sqn	Off Spurn Head
24/25 August 1940	He 111P	9/KG55	Unknown		Off Hastings
29/30 August 1940	Do 17Z	2/KG2	Unknown		Crashed in France
	He 111H	3/KG27	Spitfire	92 Sqn	Nr Hale, Cheshire
5/6 September 1940	He 111H-3	1/KG1	Blenheim	25 Sqn	Rendlesham, Suffolk
	He 111H-3	2/KG26	Unknown		Crashed in Holland
14/15 September 1940	He 111H-4	3/KG4	Blenheim	25 Sqn	Nr Sheering, Essex
17/18 September 1940	Ju 88A-1	1/KG54	Defiant	141 Sqn	Maidstone
15/16 October 1940	He 111H-4	2/KGr126	Defiant	264 Sqn	Hutton, Essex
15/16 November 1940	Do 17Z	9/KG76	Unknown		Harlow, Essex
19/20 November 1940	Ju 88A-5	3/KG54	Beaufighter	604 Sqn	Chichester
22/23 December 1940	He 111P-4	3/KG55	Defiant	141 Sqn	Etchingham, E. Sussex
15/16 January 1941	Do 17Z-2	4/KG3	Hurricane	151 Sqn	Nr Brentwood, Essex
	He 111H-5	2/KG53	Hurricane	151 Sqn	Off Canvey Island
4/5 February 1941	Do 17Z-3	7/KG2	Defiant	151 Sqn	Weldon, Northants
15/16 February 1941	He 111P-2	7/KG27	Beaufighter	604 Sqn	Haberton, Devon
17/18 February 1941	Do 17Z-3	3/KGr606	Beaufighter	219 Sqn	Windsor Great Park
25/26 February 1941	Do 17Z-2	4/KG2	Hurricane	85 Sqn	Lavenham, Suffolk
4/5 March 1941	He 111H-5	1/KG28	Beaufighter	604 Sqn	Beer Head, Devon
12/13 March 1941	He 111H-4	4/KG27	Defiant	264 Sqn	Off Hastings
	He 111P-4	5/KG55	Defiant	264 Sqn	Ockley, Surrey
	He 111P-4	6/KG55	Hurricane	96 Sqn	Widnes, Lancs
	Ju 88A-5	6/KG76	Beaufighter	604 Sqn	Kingston Deverill, Wilts
	Ju 88A-5	9/KG76	Defiant	307 Sqn	Wychbold, Worcs
13/14 March 1941	Do 17Z-2	Stab/KG2	Beaufighter	29 Sqn	Off Skegness
	He 111H-5	7/KG26	Beaufighter	219 Sqn	Shipley, Sussex
	He 111P-2	7/KG55	Beaufighter	219 Sqn	Bramdean, Hants
	He 111H-3	1/KGr100	Blenheim	600 Sqn	Dunure, Ayrshire
	Ju 88A-5	3/Ku106	Spitfire	72 Sqn	Off Amble, Northumberland
	Ju 88C-4	4/NJG2	Beaufighter	29 Sqn	Dovendale, Lincs
14/15 March 1941	He 111H-3	2/KG1	Beaufighter	29 Sqn	Off Skegness
	He 111P-4	6/KG55	Beaufighter	604 Sqn	Falfield, Glos
	Ju 88A-5	1/KGr806	Beaufighter	Unknown	Off Beachy Head
3/4 April 1941	Ju 88A-5	7/KG1	Beaufighter	604 Sqn	Off Isle of Wight
4/5 April 1941	He 111H-5	3/KG26	Beaufighter	604 Sqn	Weston-super-Mare
7/8 April 1941	He 111H-5	9/KG26	Hurricane	87 Sqn	Branscombe, Devon
	Ju 88A-5	5/KG54	Defiant	256 Sqn	Southport, Lancs
	He 111P-4	1/KG55	Beaufighter	219 Sqn	Off Worthing
8/9 April 1941	He 111H-5	9/KG26	Defiant	264 Sqn	Hitchin, Herts
	He 111H-5	2/KG27	Hurricane	151 Sqn	Warwicks
	He 111P-4	3/KG55	Hurricane	151 Sqn	Desford, Leics
	He 111P-4	8/KG55	Defiant	151 Sqn	Windsor
9/10 April 1941	He 111P-2	5/KG55	Defiant	264 Sqn	Busbridge, Surrey
	Ju 88A-5	3/KG77	Defiant	151 Sqn	Bramcote, Warwicks
	He 111H-3	2/KGr100	Beaufighter	604 Sq	Cranborne, Dorset
	Ju 88C-4	4/NJG2	Beaufighter	25 Sqn	Oakham, Rutland
	He 111H-2	2/KG1	Unknown		English Channel
	He 111P	4/KG27	Defiant	264 Sqn	Smethwick, Staffs

Date	Enemy a/c	Unit	Attacking a/c	Unit	Remarks
10/11 April 1941	Ju 88A-5	2/KG1	Hurricane	151 Sqn	Murcott, Oxford
	He 111H-5	3/KG26	Defiant	264 Sqn	Seaford, Sussex
	He 111H-5	8/KG26	Defiant	256 Sqn	Radway, Warwicks
	Ju 88A-5	1/KG54	Beaufighter	604 Sqn	Off Swanage, Dorset
	He 111P-2	9/KG55	Hurricane	151 Sqn	Kettering, Northants
	He 111H-3	3/KGr100	Beaufighter	604 Sqn	Isle of Wight
11/12 April 1941	He 111P-2	9/KG27	Defiant	307 Sqn	Lydlinch, Dorset
15/16 April 1941	Ju 88A-5	2/KG54	Beaufighter	604 Sqn	Holcombe Burnell, Devon
	He 111P-4	2/KG55	Beaufighter	604 Sqn	Off Portland Bill
	He 111P-2	8/KG55	Beaufighter	604 Sqn	Southampton
16/17 April 1941	Ju 88A-5	4/KG1	Beaufighter	219 Sqn	Cranleigh, Surrey
	He 111H-5	2/KG28	Beaufighter	219 Sqn	Wormley, Surrey
	Ju 88A-5	3/KG76	Beaufighter	219 Sqn	Wimbledon
17/18 April 1941	Ju 88C-4	4/NJG2	Unknown		Nr Peterborough
19/20 April 1941	He 111H-5	7/KG4	Hurricane	151 Sqn	Stockbury, Kent
1/2 May 1941	He 111P	4/KG27	Beaufighter	219 Sqn	Off Shoreham
2/3 May 1941	Ju 88A-6	8/KG77	Beaufighter	604 Sqn	Lyndhurst, Hants
3/4 May 1941	He 111H-5	3/KG26	Beaufighter	604 Sqn	Crowcombe, Somerset
	He 111H-5	8/KG26	Beaufighter	219 Sqn	Sidlesham, Chichester
	He 111P-2	9/KG26	Beaufighter	604 Sqn	Corton Denham, Somerset
	He 111H-4	3/KG53	Defiant	151 Sqn	Sharrington, Norfolk
	Ju 88A-6	2/KG54	Defiant	307 Sqn	Lostock Gralam, Cheshire
	Ju 88A-5	1/Ku806	Beaufighter	600 Sqn	Stoke St Michael, Somerset
4/5 May 1941	Ju 88A-5	8/KG1	Beaufighter	25 Sqn	Eastgate, Lincs
	Ju 88A-5	6/KG54	Beaufighter	604 Sqn	East Burton, Dorset
	Ju 88A-5	2/Ku106	Unknown		Idle, Bradford
5/6 May 1941	He 111H-5	1/KG54	Defiant	141 Sqn	Whorlton Park, Newcastle-on-Tyne
	Ju 88A-5	4/KG54	Beaufighter	604 Sqn	Chawleigh, Devon
6/7 May 1941	He 111H-5	7/KG27	Beaufighter	600 Sqn	Oborne, Dorset
	Ju 88A-5	5/KG30	Defiant	141 Sqn	Holy Island, N'land
	Ju 88A-5	2/Ku106	Defiant	141 Sqn	Lennoxtown, Stirling
7/8 May 1941	He 111H-5	1/KG54	Hurricane	151 Sqn	Withernsea, Yorks
	He 111P	2/KG27	Beaufighter	600 Sqn	Weston-Super-Mare
	He 111P	2/KG27	Beaufighter	600 Sqn	Isle of Wight
	He 111H-5	7/KG27	Beaufighter	604 Sqn	Weston Zoyland, Somerset
	He 111H-3	1/KG53	Defiant	255 Sqn	Scrooby, Notts
	He 111P-4	1/KG55	Defiant	265 Sqn	Stockport, Cheshire
	He 111P-4	3/KG55	Beaufighter	604 Sqn	Off Portland
	He 111P-4	3/KG55	Defiant	256 Sqn	Bagillt, Flintshire
	He 111P-4	6/KG55	Defiant	256 Sqn	Wrexham
	Ju 88A-5	3/KG76	Unknown		Gradbach, Staffs
	He 111H-2	3/KGr100	Defiant	256 Sqn	Malpas, Cheshire
	Do 17Z-10	2/NJG2	Beaufighter	25 Sqn	Carrington, Lincs
8/9 May 1941	He 111H-5	2/KG27	Beaufighter	29 Sqn	Wimbledon
	He 111H-5	4/KG53	Defiant	255 Sqn	Patrington, Hull
	He 111H-5	6/KG 53	Defiant	255 Sqn	Long Riston, Yorks
9/10 May 1941	Ju 88A-5	9/KG1	Beaufighter	219 Sqn	Off Selsey
10/11 May 1941	He 111P-2	7/KG2	Beaufighter	29 Sqn	Off Seaford, Sussex
	He 111P-2	8/KG27	Beaufighter	219 Sqn	Cranleigh, Surrey
	He 111H-5	1/KG28	Unknown		Chelmsford, Essex
	He 111H-5	3/KG53	Defiant	Unknown	Upchurch, Kent
	He 111P	9/KG55	Unknown		Withyham, E. Sussex
15/16 May 1941	Ju 88A-5	7/KG1	Beaufighter	600 Sqn	Plymtree, Devon
	He 111P-2	7/KG55	Beaufighter	219 Sqn	Sompting, Sussex

Although night attacks on the British Isles continued, the *Luftwaffe*'s bomber force was now preoccupied with operations over the Soviet Union, which was attacked on 22 June 1941. Attacks on Britain now tended to be small-scale affairs, and would never again reach the intensity of the night raids inflicted on the British people during the spring 'Blitz' of 1941.

THE TOP-SCORING *LUFTWAFFE* NIGHT FIGHTER PILOTS

Thirty German night fighter pilots scored forty or more victories in the night battle over the *Reich*. Between them, they destroyed 1,800 aircraft, the equivalent of 120 RAF Bomber Squadrons.

The Leading German Night Fighter Aces

Name	Unit(s)	Score	Remarks
Schnaufer, *Maj* Heinz-Wolfgang	NJGs 1, 4	121	
Lent, *Oberst* Helmut	NJGs 1, 2, 3	102	+8 by day k.7.10.44
Sayn-Wittgenstein, *Maj* Prince	NJGs 3,2	83	k.21.1.44
Streib, *Oberst* Werner	NJG 1	66	
Meurer, *Hauptmn* Manfred	NJGs 1,5,	65	k.21.1.44
Radusch, *Oberst* Gunther	NJGs 1,3,5,2	64	
Rokker, *Hauptmn* Heinz	NJG 2	64	
Schonert, *Maj* Rudolf	NJGs 1,2,5,100	64	
Zorner, *Maj* Paul	NJGs 2,3,5,100	59	
Raht, *Hauptmn* Gerhard	NJG 2	58	
Herget, *Maj* Wilhelm	NJGs 4,3,71	57	+14 by day
Becker, *Hauptmn* Martin	NJGs 3,4,6	57	
Francsi, *Oberlt* Gustave	NJG 100	56	
Kraft, *Hauptmn* Josef	NJGs 4,5,1,6	56	
Struning, *Hauptmn* Heinz	NJGs 2,1	56	k.24.12.44
Frank, *Hauptmn* Hans-Dieter	NJG 1	55	k.27.9.43
Vinke, *Feldwbl* Heinz	NJG 1	54	k.26.2.44
Geiger, *Hauptmn* August	NJG 1	53	k.27.9.43
Lutje, *Oberstlt* Herbert	NJGs 1,6	53	
Drewes, *Maj* Martin	NJG 1	52	
Hoffmann, *Maj* Werner	NJGs 3,5	52	
Lippe-Weissenfeld, *Maj* Prince	NJGs 2,1,5	51	k.12.3.44
Welter, *Oberlt* Kurt	JG 300, NJG 11	50+	
Greiner, *Hauptmn* Hermann	NJG 1	50	
Kollack, *Stabsfeldwbl* Reinhard	NJGs 1,4	49	
Becker, *Hauptmn* Ludwig	NJGs 2, 1	46	k.26.2.43
Frank, *Leutnant* Rudolf	NJG 3	45	k.26.4.44
Gildner, *Oberlt* Paul	NJG 1	44	k.24.2.43
Knacke, *Hauptmn* Reinhold	NJG 1	44	k.3.2.43
Jabs, *Oberstlt* Hans-Joachim	NJG 1	28	+22 by day

BIBLIOGRAPHY

Aders, G. *History of the German Night Fighter Force*. Jane's, 1979.

Ashmore, Maj-Gen E.B. *Air Defence*. Longmans, 1929.

Bekker, Cajus. *The Luftwaffe War Diaries*. Macdonald, 1966.

Brandon, Sqn Ldr L. *Night Flyer*. William Kimber, 1969.

Brew, A. *The Defiant File*. Air-Britain, 1996.

Chisholm, R. *Cover of Darkness*. Chatto & Windus, 1953.

Cole, C. and Cheesman, F. *The Air Defence of Britain 1914–18*. Putnam 1984.

Darlington, R. *Night Hawk*. William Kimber, 1985.

Delve, K. *Nightfighter. The Battle for the Night Skies*. Arms & Armour Press, 1995.

Gentil, R. *Trained to Intrude*. Bachman & Turner, 1974.

Gunston, Bill. *Night Fighters. A Development and Combat History*. PSL 1976.

Held, W. and Nauroth, H. *The Night Fighters. German Fighters in World War II: a Photographic History of the German Nachtjäger 1940-1945*. Schiffer Publications (USA) 1995.

Held, W. and Nauroth, H. *The Defence of the Reich. Hitler's Nightfighter Planes and Pilots*. Arco (USA) 1982.

Hermann, H. *On Eagles' Wings*. Guild Publishing 1991.

Hinchcliffe, P. *The Other Battle. Luftwaffe Night Aces versus Bomber Command*. Airlife 1996.

Howard-Williams, J. *Night Intruder*. David & Charles 1976.

Hunt, L. *Defence Until Dawn. The Story of No 488 (NZ) Squadron*. Crecy Books 1993.

Jackson, R. *Air War over Korea*. Airlife 1998.

Jackson, R. *Air War over Flanders, 1914–18*. Airlife, 1999.

Jackson, R. *The High Cold War*. PSL, 1998.

Johnen, W. *Duel Under the Stars. A German Night Fighter Pilot in the Second World War*. Crecy Books 1994.

Lindsay, R. *Service History of the Gloster Javelin Mks 7 to 9R*. Privately published and undated.

Middlebrook, M. and Everitt, C. *The Bomber Command War Diaries*. Viking 1985.

Nauroth, H. and Held, W. *Messerschmitt Bf110 Zerstörer*. Motorbuch, 1978.

Philpott, B. *Meteor*. PSL 1986.

Price, A. *Battle over the Reich*. Ian Allan 1973.

Rawnsley, C.F. and Wright, R. *Night Fighter*. Collins, 1957.

Robinson, A. *Nightfighter. A Concise History of Nightfighting Since 1914*. Ian Allan 1988.

Spooner, T. *Night Fighter Ace*. Sutton Publishing 1997. (Story of Wg Cdr Bob Braham.)

INDEX

AIRFIELDS/AIRSTRIPS

PERSONNEL

INDEX